ECONOMICS OF TAXATION: Theory and Application

ECONOMICS OF TAXATION:
Theory and Application

B. MISHRA

AKANSHA PUBLISHING HOUSE
NEW DELHI-110002

AKANSHA PUBLISHING HOUSE
4649-B/21, Ansari Road
Darya Ganj, New Delhi - 110 002
Email: ektabooks@yahoo.com
Ph.: 23263193/9811582579
Fax: 011-23263193

ECONOMICS OF TAXATION: Theory and Application

First Published 2006
ISBN 81-8370-062-4

PRINTED IN INDIA

Published by M.P. Misra for Akansha Publishing House, New Delhi and Printed at Aryan Enterprises, Delhi

CONTENTS

PREFACE

Demand for increased public expenditure due to enhanced political consciousness and implementation of investment programmes through mechanism(s) infected with diseconomies are the two important forces among several others to put increased pressure on the fiscal resources available within a state. Short-term measures undertaken by a Sate viz., dependence on federal transfers and resorting to overdraft evidently has their respective detrimental implications on fiscal health of the state. The inadequacy in generating their own sources of revenue to meet the ever increasing public expenditure growth in these states has given rise to a volatile fiscal situation. Given this backdrop, the present work makes an attempt to study the extent to which the revenue capacity of these state's tax system has been realized and to assess the overall success of government measures to increase revenue potentialities of the tax system and Orissa's overall capacities to raise the tax-income ratio overtime. The remedial approach pervasively suggested by the contemporary fiscal strategists to tackle the ever-increasing fiscal gap moves towards attaining an appropriate degree of financial self reliance. Thus, the obvious solution of fiscal restructuring dwells on an in-depth understanding of the fiscal system of a state particularly on a temporal analysis of the indicators that throw light on the performance of a tax system in respect of two objectives: (i) siphoning off into the state exchequer the collection of revenue without endangering the incentive for private savings and investment and (ii) helping to release resources for private investment by reducing private consumption.

By applying four indicators, viz. compound growth rate, marginal tax rates, and elasticity and buoyancy coefficients to the Orissa's tax structure, the present book tries to assess the fiscal performances of the state of Orissa with respect to the above two objectives.

In carrying out the work, I have benefited a great extent from the various studies carried out by various researchers and scholars at International and National level on the tax responsiveness. I gracefully acknowledge my intellectual debt to all of them.

I hope that the present book will prove to be of immense value to the post-graduate students, Research scholars, fiscal analysts and the taxation theorists. I believe that the book will seek to offer a guideline for further intellectual exercises on the same line.

I would like to place on record my deep sense of indebtedness to Prof. T. Mathew, from whom I learnt and developed an interest for Public Finance.

My obligations to Prof. K. B. Das, Department of Analytical and applied Economics, Utkal University, Bhubaneswar, who have been the guiding spirit and the beacon light in all my endeavors, shall remain ever unpaid.

I owe a a special debt of gratitude to Prof. E.D.Thomas, Prof. S.K.Mishra, Prof. P.Nayak and Dr. P.S. Suresh who have helped and encouraged me in various ways while preparing the manuscript.

I find no words to give my innermost feelings for my wife (Sujata) and my son (Echo) for their silent sacrifices without which, I could not have dreamt of completing this work.

I dedicate this humble work to all of teachers who taught me Economics.

B. Mishra

LIST OF TABLES

LIST OF FIGURES

CHAPTER - I

INTRODUCTION

BACKGROUND OF THE STUDY

One of the major problems facing the developing countries is the attainment of rapid economic development. The developmental theorists argue in general that the obvious requirement for development is a steady and rapid rate of capital accumulation. The capital accumulation does not take place in vacuum. Capital accumulation depends on the dynamics of the economy supported by both internal and external stimulus. Therefore, in a developing economy the question of achieving a desired rate of capital accumulation remains elusive. Unlike the developed economies, where most of the capital accumulation takes place through the market mechanism in the presence of a huge amount of capital goods, capital accumulation in a developing economy, does not usually take place through any such market mechanism, because, capital goods do not flow constantly to the market in the absence of a sound infrastructural footing. Therefore, it is often argued that their governments must be responsible for most of the capital accumulation. The investment in the basic infrastructural set up (as Goode (1963)[1], argues, constitute as a necessary pre-condition for rapid increase in innovation and capital formation in manufacturing, commerce and agriculture) besides necessiating large quantum of capital deployments do not result in quick and direct returns as to attract private individuals to come forward to invest, thereby shouldering a part of Government's responsibility in this regard.

One important corollary that follows from the above argument is that, the Government, in a developing economy, has to play an important role in promoting economic development. In doing so, the Government has to cope up with the problem of increasing pressure to raise its rate of spending in many fields.

To augment the pace of economic development, it is necessary that resources should be generated through various fiscal measures. Resource for development purposes may be obtained either from internal or external sources, or from both. Given the inherent institutional setup it is the general weakness of the developing countries to withstand the competition from developed countries, it forces them to pay greater attention to the maximum possible exploitation of internal resources. In the light of the above discussion, we think it imperative to confine our discussion to the fiscal problems associated with mobilizing resources from internal sources. The alternative ways of augmenting internal sources are : (i) Increase the savings either voluntarily through a reduction in current consumption or involuntarily through additional taxation, compulsory lending to the Government, or "forced savings" through inflation, (ii) by the utilization of the `disguised unemployed labour' in the productive work and, (iii) through a combination of all these schemes.

Any substantial increase in savings through a voluntary reduction in current consumption is not very likely to occur in an economy like ours, where the average income per head is pathetically low[2].

Depressing consumption and generating "forced savings" through inflationary process is not an efficient method of resource mobilization for development needs[3]. For, as

Dorrance argues, "inflation is likely to evoke forces which both diminish the resources available for development and reduce the true effectiveness of those funds which continue to flow into investment. Savings is likely to be lower than under stable monetary conditions and to take forms which lead to lessening of forces of economic criteria, in the choice of investment"[4]. Further, it has been shown by Sinharay that in the case of India, during the period of the first two five-year plans, there has been an "absence of any relationship between inflation and accelerated economic development"[5]. The nature of the relationship between these two phenomena does not seem to have been altered in any significant degree during the subsequent plan periods too.

Utilization of the "disguised unemployed labour" for development needs is a very attractive theoretical proposition. But operationally it is not a feasible one, especially in a democratic set up economy like ours because, the administrative cost in implementing the scheme of activating the saving potential implied in disguised unemployment may outweigh the likely benefit that the economy may derive from the scheme.

Mobilizing resources through compulsory lending to the government was tried in India through the Annuity Deposit Scheme introduced in 1964-65. The scheme was, however, given up from 1969-70, owing to its benefits not being commensurate with the expenses in effort, time and money required to administer the scheme. The scheme has been re-introduced in the supplementary budget of 1974-75. However, high marginal propensity to consume and presence of a large non-monetized sector in the economy has created considerable difficulties in the mobilization of resources from compulsory lending.

Thus, the feasible method of resource mobilisation for an economy like India for the purposes of development lies in the instrument of additional taxation. It may be mentioned that over the last three decades the tax system, both in its direct and indirect levies has been overhauled and refashioned so as to make it a suitable instrument for furthering the objectives of economic development[6].

In a federation like India, the financing of the state development plans depends to a large extent on the mobilisation of resources by the state Governments mainly through an effective exercise of their power of taxation. Efforts made in this direction from time to time have not uniformly succeeded. Being federal in structure, the state Governments has limited statutory powers to levy taxes to finance its various infrastructural facilities and welfare programmes. This may be ascribed to the fact that while bulk of the federal revenue has been derived from more elastic sources, implying that the revenue from these taxes increases proportionately, if not faster than income, the sources of the state Government are relatively less elastic, as reported by Rao (1992)[7].

With the expansion of the Governmental activities, the magnitude of plan expenditures of the state Governments have increased tremendously which in turn has given rise to the need for a rapid increase in revenue. It is expected that, the sources of revenue should grow automatically at the required rate. But the experiences of most of the state Governments in India negate the above proposition. As a result of which, this has created a widening gap between the state's expenditure responsibilities on the one hand and available resources on the other, thereby giving rise to the problem of attaining an appropriate degree of financial self-reliance on the part of the most of the state Governments in India. However it is also felt that to a large extent, the financial problems of the states arise owing to lack of efforts on their own part to raise additional resources. On this account, the need for an indepth analysis of the tax-efforts at the state level has been felt for quite some time.

Although the financial problem is one common to central as well as to state Governments, the financial constraints imposed on state Governments in India under the constitution in practice define their options more narrowly. In India, the emergence of a situation is evident in which, some states are excessively dependent on federal transfers, while others resort extensively to overdrafts, which can be attributed either to the failure on the part of the state Governments in tapping all the productive sources of revenue or to the fact that a 'critical limit' as regards to tax effort as well as taxable capacity has already reached in case of most the states. This excessive dependence of the states on the centre is not all conducive to the development of sound federal fiscal conventions. This scenario makes a strong case for analysing the states fiscal condition.

With this background in mind, an attempt has been made in this work to study the intricacies of state's finance from two angles.

Firstly, a general resource crunch has been signaled by the Federal Government in the recent times. In fact, Union Government has been under tremendous pressure to prune expenditure in order to reduce its deficit. This has necessitated reduction on outlays on the centrally sponsored development schemes in the states on the one hand and on the other, this has led to a major cut in subsidies and grants to the states. Thus, the outlays of the states have been substantially affected, thereby forcing the State Governments to postpone some of its developmental plan programmes. As a result of which the existing pattern of resource allocation of the financial resources between the union of India and its constituent units has generated imbalances between the revenue capacities and the needs of the States much to the detriment of the backward states of India. In this particular context, a successful attempt is made at enquiring into the nature, causes and dimensions of such maladjustments and imbalances, taking Orissa as typically backward state.

Secondly, the state's fiscal position in general has not been encouraging all together. Most distressing feature of state's finances has been growing deficit in recent years in most of the states for which such an analysis was undertaken. A recent study by Rao[8], shows that most of these states had surplus of about 1.2 percent of States' Domestic Product till mid-seventies. But, in late eighties, most of the states have shown deficit of about 1 percent of State Domestic Product. This study, which includes almost all the States of Indian Union shows that the situation from the surplus to the deficit may have resulted for the following two reasons. (i) these states have shown high growth of revenue expenditure of about 18 percent per annum. This may be attributed to increasing subsidies, both direct and indirect, increasing Wage Bills complemented by increased expenditure on goods and services utilized by State Governments. (ii) The interest liability of these states have been growing at an alarming average rate of about 23 percent per annum. This may be attributed to an emphasis on having large plan outlays without commensurate resources, which resulted in financing plans through borrowings. As a result, most of these states have experienced explosive cycles of revenue-expenditure growth. To counter balance this, we believe, that the State Governments may have to resort to either of the following two alternatives to seek higher revenue.

(i) The first recourse before the State Governments may be to re-structure their tax system in such a way so as to yield more revenue. But, the manner in which increasing revenue may be realised through a properly structured tax system at any given time is largely conditioned not only by the various socio-economic and political factors, but also by the efficiency of the State's administrative apparatus, which sets important limits to the ambit, pattern and structure of taxation (Lakdawala, D. T. and Nambiar, K. V., 1972)[9].

(ii) The second alternative that can be spelled out runs in terms of improving the revenue elasticity and buoyancy of the tax structure, so that the tax system will show an automatic response to the growth of the Net State's Domestic Product. The high degree of tax responsiveness to our view may set a limit to an 'optimal level' of taxation on the one hand and to an 'optimal level' of tax effort on the other. To what extent, the State's Government can achieve or have already achieved this objective is an open question.

Therefore, the present study is a modest effort in this direction to find out a suitable answer to the above question, by taking into account this second aspect of the problem of State's finances.

In order to evolve a rational policy of taxation, it is necessary to have an idea about the extent of additional tax effort needed to increase the revenue of the Government, that is to say by relating the Government's tax effort to the elasticity and buoyancy of tax or tax sensitivity formula. Since, R. F. Bretherton (1937) made the first comprehensive method for measuring the elasticity of British tax structure[10], several studies have been made[11] in India at the all India level for measuring the elasticity and buoyancy of the tax structure. Further, there have also been studies on this subject at the state's level, particularly pertaining to Assam and Punjab[12]. A study about the elasticity and buoyancy of taxation at the aggregate level is no doubt useful. However, wide variations in the levels of living as also in the tax efforts made by various States call for a more specific enquiry at the State level.

Although, taxation falls within the purview of both the Central and the State Government, it has often been said, that the State's are at a disadvantage vis-a-vis the Union in the distribution of tax powers. In support of this view, it is pointed out that the tax sources assigned to the States are inelastic whereas those assigned to the Union are elastic. But, the analysis presented by Rao has revealed that Union taxes are no more elastic in relation to income than State taxes. But the Union Government has been able to improve its revenues to a much greater extent than the State Governments on account of its willingness to utilise its tax sources more intensively[13]. However, not many serious studies appear to have been done in this sphere at the State level. A modest effort here is an attempt to study and understand some problems of revenue potentialities of the tax system and the State's overall capacities to raise the tax-income ratio overtime in Orissa.

PROBLEM FORMULATION

It is evident from the above discussion that most of the State Governments in Indian Federation face severe budgetary pressures with rising demand for expenditures. Further, it is generally felt that to a large extent, the financial problems of the States arise from their lack of tax efforts, i.e., their failure to mobilise adequate resources from sources within their own jurisdiction. As a result of which, the financial dependence of the States on the Union Government has been on the increase in recent years. However, it is felt that, the resources available to the States under present dispensation are not adequate for meeting their requirements. The present study intends to accomplish this by analysing fiscal position of Orissa.

Orissa is comparatively a backward state, where agriculture is the predominant sector, providing means of livelihood to more than 80 percent of the population. Though significant development has taken place in some sphere since Independence, access to opportunities for a 'reasonably minimum' standard of living in Orissa in one of the lowest in the country. More than two-thirds of its population lives below the poverty line and where the state's own tax revenue contributes hardly 26.6 percent of the total tax receipts of the state. Further, the tax revenue constitutes 24.09 percent of the aggregate revenue of the state. In a state like Orissa, where the state's own tax revenue contributes no more than 5.2 percent of the state's income and the aggregate Government expenditures constitutes 53.3 percent of the state's income, it is worthwhile to study the various aspects of the effects of state taxation on equity, revenue and efficiency in production and distribution. However, our study has not gone into some of these aspects of fiscal policy, as its primary aim is specific to the analysis of elasticity and buoyancy.

Thus, the overall picture that emerges is that, the tax generating capacity of the state of Orissa does not cope up with its increased public expenditure programmes, for achieving a desirable rate of economic progress. This exhibits clearly the low level of tax efforts measures on the part of the state government in the overall scheme of resource mobilisation for developmental purposes. As a result of which, economic backwardness has been the resultant outcome.

In order to solve these problems, the tax system must be arranged in such a way so as to produce the best overall effects in terms of sustinable economic growth with stability. If conceived wisely and used judicionsly it can become a very effective instrument of policy and a part of general programme of development and the resources required for it.

Based on the above logic, a basic argument underlying this study is that if Orissa's tax policy is to serve the ends of economic development, it should aim to attain atleast two objectives[14]. The tax system as an instrument of resource mobilisation should aim at (i) in siphoning off into the state exchequer as much revenues as can be gathered in the tax net (without endangering the incentives for private savings and investment) and (ii) in helping to release resources for private (or public) investment by reducing current consumption.

It is thought imperative to apply six indicators to assess Orissa's performance with respect to the above two objectives.

These indicators are: the buoyancy and elasticity, the compound growth rate and the marginal tax rate, the tax ratio and tax effort. Of these six indicators, the compound growth rate and marginal tax rates are less significant analytically, since, they do not take into account taxable capacity. Among the remaining four measures, the tax ratio and the tax effort measures generally do not indicate, whether or not the tax structure is responsive to changes in state income overtime. Thus, we are left to the choice of applying the elasticity and buoyancy coefficients to the tax structure so as to assess directly the efficiency of state tax measure. So, it is clear that, if the state's tax structure satisfies two conditions, namely, that: (i) the buoyancy of taxes is substantially higher than unity; and (ii) the elasticity is equal to or marginally greater than unity, then it can be said that the state tax system has performed satisfactorily, given its relative taxable capacity. But an attempt is made in this work to apply all the six indicators to ascertain the efficacy of he state's tax system. The effectiveness of Orissa's tax system is assessed in the context of these six norms with a major emphasis on the analytical tools of tax elasticity and buoyancy.

On the state level, tax revenue may change through automatic response of the tax yield to changes in State Income and, or, through the imposition of new taxes, revision of the rates, stricter tax compliance and other administrative measures backed by legal action. Changes in the tax yield resulting from modifying such tax parameters (i.e., rates, bases etc.) are called discretionary changes, which may incidentally involve some legislative action. Changes in the tax yield flowing from the combined effects of automatic responses as well as discretionary changes constitute the "buoyancy" of a tax. On the other hand, with tax parameters held constant (i.e., discretionary changes being removed) automatic changes in the tax yield resulting from variations in the state income measures the "elasticity" of a tax or a tax system.

The need for undertaking such an analysis for the state taxation in Orissa arises due to the following reasons.

Since the buoyancy coefficient compares the actual growth of tax revenue with the growth in State Income, it indicates the following resultant outcome. First, it helps in assessing the overall success of Government's measures to increase tax revenue. Secondly, to the extent that the buoyancy is low, it would suggest a need for devising a tax structure which would overcome the deficiencies. Thirdly, on the basis of such study, the state Government can estimate the probable tax revenue with unchanged base and the rate of tax, consequent on more increase in the State Income.

The elasticity coefficient on the other hand, indicates the inherent responsiveness of a tax system to changes in the State Income and also it reflects, how far the revenue potential of a given tax system has been realized.

It is against this theoretical problem, a humble attempt is being made in this study, to throw some light on the problems of estimating elasticity and buoyancy of the state taxes in Orissa, in order to determine the degree of responsiveness of the state taxes to the state's Domestic Product. This will exhibit the relative degree of efficiency of state tax measures and will indicate the extent of additional tax efforts needed to increase the revenue of the Government.

SCOPE AND OBJECTIVES OF THE STUDY

The study covers a period of thirty-three years, from 1962 to 1994. This is a period during which the state economy has passed through phases of both upswing and downswing owing to wide fluctuations in its agricultural sector. During this period, the tax policies of the state Government have also undergone substantial changes. Keeping this general problem in view, an attempt has been made in this work to study in details the following aspects of state taxes.

(i) An assessment of the overall success of the Government measures to increase Government revenue.

(ii) An analysis of the growth of tax revenue consequent on the growth of Gross State Domestic Product and, to determine the extent to which Orissa's tax system is responsive to changes in State Income overtime.

(iii) To measure the extent to which the revenue potential of Orissa's tax system has been realised.

(iv) An enquiry into the share of taxes in the state's contribution towards the finances required for its own development; analysis of the drawbacks, if any, in the state's tax system and a consequential investigation into the need and feasibility of an alternative tax system.

However, the main focus of the study as mentioned earlier is the analysis of elasticity and buoyancy of the tax system as a whole and of each individual tax to changes in tax base and in the State Income.

SOURCES AND LIMITATIONS OF DATA

The study has been based primarily on the secondary sources of data. The major sources of data for the study are the annual budgets of the Orissa state Government, including their memorandum submitted to various Finance Commissions for the year 1961-62 to 1993-94. We have also used wherever possible, the budgetary data relating to India, as published from time to time in the Reserve Bank of India Bulletin and the Reserve Bank of India's Annual Reports on Currency and Finance. The figures on Net State Domestic Product were obtained from the Estimates of State Domestic product as published by the Directorate of Economics and Statistics, Government of Orissa. Further, certain relevant data have been culled from various issues of Economic Survey of Orissa, published by the Government of Orissa for the entire period of our study. It is found that some data necessary to estimate different components were not available in the exact form in which they were wanted. In such cases, the data base was prepared by using arithmetic adjustments.

METHODOLOGY

The data has been analysed with the help of suitable statistical techniques and the results obtained have been subjected to relevant economic logic.

Simple regression equations are fitted to the data (by the method of least square) to estimate the trends and fluctuations in revenues and expenditures of the Government of Orissa for the period under study. The different items or broad heads of revenues and expenditures having thus regressed on time, the variations explained by the time factor have been found out. To study the shifts in the relative shares of various taxes and non-tax sources in state's own revenue, the present work makes use of the statistical technique of time series analysis. Specific techniques and measures are described fully as and when used. To analyse the relative growth of different sources of tax and non-tax revenues, compound growth rates were calculated by using the formula:

$$Y = ae^{rt}$$

where,

Y is the revenue from a particular tax or non-tax source and t is the time period and r is the growth rate. The least square estimate of the above formula has been worked out to arrive at the growth rate figures.

As the main focus of the study is on the analysis of elasticity and buoyancy of the tax system and of individual taxes, the proposed method has been geared to that purpose. This study suggests the use of an alternative to the conventional method. The new method, developed in this study is described in details in chapter 5.

CHAPTER PLAN

The topical organization of the book is as follows. For the purpose of expositional convenience and systematic analysis, the book has been divided into six parts namely (1) Introduction, (2) Review of literature, (3) The trends and patterns of taxation and public expenditure, (4) Fiscal anamolies of Orissa including the central transfers, which is set against the background of planned development, (5) Elasticity and buoyancy of state tax system as a whole and that of individual taxes, and (6) prospects, summary and conclusions.

The first chapter is intended to be Introductory in nature. In this chapter, the book addresses to the intricate problems and issues involved in the state finance. Besides, this chapter also incorporates a description of the methodology followed in this study and the sources and limitations of data.

The second chapter is devoted to the review of some of the important works done on the subject. An attempt has been made in this chapter to give a comprehensive account of the major conceptual and empirical issues relating to the analysis of elasticity and buoyancy of taxation.

The third chapter is concerned with an analytical and critical evaluation of the tax-expenditure policies, where we have made an attempt to assess the overall success of the Government measures to increase Government Revenue to finance its increased developmental expenditures. Further, a brief analysis of the growth of tax revenue consequent upon the growth of gross state domestic product is being carried out in this chapter, in order to know the extent to which orissa's tax system is responsive to changes in state income over time.

In Chapter four, an attempt is made to examine the problems of resource constraint and prospects of internal resource mobilization in the State during the last thirty-three years of planning. The purpose of this is to present an overview of all the sources of state finances for determining the degree of financial dependence of the state on the Union Government, which has tremendously increased in recent times. An attempt has been made in this chapter to determine the extent to which Orissa is financially self-reliant in mobilising adequate resources from sources within its own jurisdiction.

Chapter five, reviews the progressiveness and productivity of Orissa's taxes in terms of the indicators noted earlier. This chapter is divided into three parts. In the first part, an attempt is made to develop an alternative model of elasticity and buoyancy for measuring the responsiveness of Orissa's tax system by taking into account the difficulties associated with the estimation of elasticity and buoyancy of the tax system. An estimation of elasticity and buoyancy of the state tax system as a whole is carried out in section two. And, in section three, we present an analysis of elasticity and buoyancy of individual state taxes.

The final chapter is devoted to a summary of our analysis and its conclusion following from it. An attempt is made to evaluate the existing pattern of the tax system in the state and of its implications for tax policy in the light of the findings of our study.

NOTES AND REFERENCES

1. Goode, R. B.; "Taxation and Economic Development", in Morgan, T.; Betz, G. W.; and Choudhary, N. (eds); Readings in Economic Development, Belmont; wordsworth publishing Co., 1963.
2. Even among the affluent few, in an economy like India, this tendency for the marginal propensity to consume to increase with increasing incomes may further be stimulated by the 'international demonstration effect', which through the modern means of communication, exercises a very powerful influence on the consumption pattern of less developed countries.
3. An implicit assumption of the growth propelling nature of forced savings is that there is a direct link between credit expansion and investment, that is to say, additional command

over resources created by inflationary expansion of money supply is assumed to be used to increase capital goods production. The genuineness of forced savings (i.e., they are the result of forced reduction in consumption) is also to be emphasized, for finding real finances (resources) for developmental purpose is entirely different from finding increased money for it. No Government with control over the Central Bank will find it difficult to get the necessary amount of domestic money, but real resources can come only out of the sacrifice (through postponement or curtailment) of current consumption for the sake of further benefit.

4. Dorrence, Graeme S.; "The Effects of Inflation on Economic Development", IMF staff papers, vol. 17, No. 2, March, 1963.
5. Sinharay, M.; "On Government Expenditure and Economic Development of India", Economic studies, March 1964, pp. 459-466.
6. The committees which (and individuals, who) investigated the Indian tax system such as, the Taxation Enquiry Commission in 1954, Nicholas Kaldor in 1956, the Central Excise Reorganization Committee in 1963, S. Boothalingam in 1968, the Direct Taxes Enquiry Committee in 1971, Raj committee in 1972, Indirect Taxation Enquiry committee in 1976, Chelliah committee Report in 1987, all these had the restructuring of the Indian tax system as the object of their exercise so as to make it the potent and flexible instrument of plan implementation and revision in the manifold interpretations of the terms.
7. Rao, M. G.; "Proposal for State Level Budgetary Reforms", paper presented at IIDs seminar on Fiscal Discipline and Fiscal Consolidation at the central and state level IIDs, Calcutta, February 19, 1992 (mimeo).
8. Ibid.,; pp. 7-10.
9. Lakdawala, D.T. and Nambiar, K.V.,; "Commodity Taxation in India", Ahmedabad, Sardar Patel Institute of Economic and Social Research, 1972, p. 1.

10. Bretherton, R. F.; 'The sensitivity of Taxes To Fluctuations of Trade', in Econometrica, vol. V, (1937), pp. 171-183.

11. For illustrative purposes mention may be made here of some of the well known studies on the subject in India.

    (a) Lakdawala, D.T. and Khambadkone; "The Sensitivity of Central Taxes : 1948-49 to 1954-55", The Economic Weekly, December 5th, 1959, pp. 1933-1940.

    (b) Sahota, G. S.; "Indian Tax Structure and Economic Development", Bombay, Asia Publishing house, 1961, see pp. 12-13 and 19 and 62-65.

    (c) Rao, V. G.; "The Responsiveness of Tax system in India", New Delhi, Allied Publishers Pvt. Ltd., 1979, see pp. 35-73.

    (d) Rao, K. B. K.; "Does the Indian Tax Policy Have a Rational" Margin, vol. 4, No. 3, April 1972, pp. 164-168.

    (e) Reddy, K. N.; "Inter - state Tax Effort", Economic and Political weekly, vol. X, No. 50, Dec. 13, 1975, pp. 1916-17.

    (f) Nambiar, K. V. and Rao, M. Govinda,; "Tax Performance of States", Economic and political weekly, vol. VII, No. 21, May 20, 1972, p. 1036.

    (g) Chelliah, Raja J. and Sinha, Narain,; "Measurement of Tax Effort of State Government 1973-76", New Delhi, National Institute of Public Finance and Policy, 1983, p. 4.

    (h) Jain, M. M.; "Income Elasticity of Indian Tax Structure 1955-56 to 1965-66", Economic and political weekly, vol. IV, No. 18, May 3, 1969, pp. 769-71.

    (i) Sury, M. M.; "Buoyancy and Elasticity of Union Excise Revenue in India : 1950-51 to 1980-81", unpublished Ph.D. thesis, University of Delhi, 1985.

12. Bansal, R. K.; "Raising Additional Resources in the States", New Delhi, Atlantic Publishers and Distributors, 1988, see pp. 39-136.

    Das, S. K.; "Dynamics of Taxation in A Developing Economy

(with special reference to Assam) : 1964-65 to 1978-79," Guwahati, Omson Publication, 1987. see pp. 132-213

13. Rao, K. B. K.; "Income Elasticity of Central and State taxes", Margin, vol. I, No. 3, April 1969, pp. 11-21.

14. Alternative statements of the objectives of development oriented taxation policy discussed in theliterature include :

    (i) The Promotion of Distributive Justice, (T. Barna, Redistribution of income through public Finance, Oxford Claredan Press, 1945); (Richard, M. Bird Public Finance and Inequality, Finance and Development, March, 1947, pp. 2-4).

    (ii) The Promotion of Industry; (Robert, B. Bangs, Planning and Economic Development : Fiscal policy for emerging countries, University of Chicago Press, 1968, p. 119).

    (iii) The Rationalization of Taxation Structure, (Benjamin Higgins, Economic Development : Principles, Problems and Policies, Central Book Depot, Allahabad, 1966, P. 509).

    (iv) The expansion of employment opportunities, (Bird, R. M. and Oldman, O. (eds.), Readings on Taxation in Developing Countries, John Hopkins Press, 1972).

    (v) The gradual reduction of reliance on indirect taxes, (Due, John F., Indirect Taxation in Developing Countries, John Hopkins Press, 1970; Government of India, Report of Indirect Taxation Enquiry Committee, part 1, October 1977, p. 2).

    (vi) The mobilization of savings or surplus mobilization, (Kaldor, Nicholas; Taxation for Economic Development, Journal of modern African studies, vol. 1, No. 1, 1963, pp. 7-11; Chelliah, Raja J., fiscal policy in underdeveloped countries, George Allen and Unwin (India) Ltd., 1969, p. 66).

CHAPTER - II

REVIEW OF LITERATURE

INTRODUCTION

In the previous chapter it has been pointed out that in the wake of fiscal crisis in recent years, most of the state Governments have increasingly began to restructure their tax system to seek higher revenue or to improve the revenue elasticity and buoyancy of the tax structure in order to compel the tax system to show an automatic response to the growth of the Net State's domestic product so as to help in siphoning off into the state exchequer as much revenue as can be gathered in the tax net in order to finance the increasing developmental expenditures. In working out a developmental plan which implicitly takes into account the tax ratios and the tax efforts; a major question that always arises is how much tax and non-tax revenues can a country/ state reasonably expect to raise and what sources should be tapped? Systematic tax elasticity and buoyancy estimation and comparisons may be illuminating and a number of recent empirical studies may be helpful in identifying the ideal tax and non-tax structures in the light of the parameters they have based their analysis.

REVIEW OF LITERATURE

The aim of this chapter is to review some of the important works done in India and abroad on the substantive aspect of the present study namely, the analysis of elasticity and buoyancy of taxation. This chapter is divided into two sections. Section-I of this chapter concentrates on a brief assessment of the major studies conducted at the international level on the subject for focusing on the relative significance of the factors analysed. And in section-II an attempt has been made to give a comprehensive account of the major works done in India by various researchers relating to the analysis of elasticity and buoyancy of taxation, and the problems that are encountered with the analysis.

SECTION - I

INTERNATIONAL STUDIES ON ELASTICITY AND BUOYANCY

A number of studies have been carried out in recent years which estimate the elasticity and buoyancy of taxation. Comparatively, all most all past studies have employed the regression analysis approach, using cross-sectional data.

Earlier Bretherton (1937) estimated the elasticity by calculating the percentage of change in tax to percentage of change in national income. His measurement of elasticity, (which he denotes as sensitivity index) of the British tax structure with given tax rate and coverage of the tax base by using the formula:

$$Et = \frac{\Delta T}{\Delta Y} \times \frac{Y}{T} \approx 1$$

Where, T = tax yield,

Y = National income and

Δ= changes in the respective variables.

The resultant policy prescription that follows from Bretherton's approach is that if the elasticity of a tax structure is equal to unity, the tax structure is destabilizing and, if it is greater than unity it is stabilizing. Hicks (1938) followed Bretherton, while Edelberg (1940) in his estimating equation of tax, introduced new elements like employment and trend, instead of national income, asserting that there is direct correlation between income and employment, which was proved wrong by the later empiricists. By taking into account three variables, namely, tax yield (T), Time (X) and employment (N), he tried to establish a functional relationship between them, which can be written as :

$$T = k\,X^{b}\,N^{c} \qquad (1)$$

Where, k, b and c are constants. Then, he found out simple and multiple correlation values between these variables and finally he worked out the elasticity of (T) in relation to (X) and (N) as:

$$e = \frac{\Delta T}{\Delta Y} \times \frac{Y}{T} \qquad (2)$$

Where, e is the elasticity.

Later, Groves and Khan (1952) undertook an analysis in the line of Bretherton by using a multiplicative model to show constancy of income elasticity of tax and asserted that extraneous influence of change in tax rate or tax base contributed to the realization of tax, although they failed in their attempt to separate them. They defined income elasticity as :

$$(\Delta\ T/T)\ /\ (\Delta\ Y/Y)$$

where, T was defined as tax revenue and Y as income variable. Assuming constant elasticity, they derived the coefficient through direct application of the revenue function, which runs in terms of :

$$\text{Log } T = \text{Log } a + b \text{ Log } Y$$

Where, a = Constant term,

T = Tax revenue and

Y = National income.

They asserted that in a least square fit of the above equation on time series data, the regression co-efficient gives the percent change in (T) that accompanies a one percent change in Y. Their study did not take in to account the influence of the extraneous factors such as discretionary changes in tax rates and tax bases. Accordingly, they confined their analysis to those particular states, where there occurred no discretionary changes in the tax parameters. Groves and Khan further avoided this difficulty by assuming unit elasticity of tax revenue with respect to tax rates, i.e.

$$(\Delta t_i / t_i) / (\Delta r_i / r_i) = 1$$

where, t_i was defined as the revenue from the 'i'th tax and r_i as the corresponding tax rate.

The short comings of these methods are: that it is difficult to find any economy where the tax rates remain unchanged for a longer period of time. Secondly, the approach remains silent about the factors that determine $\Delta T/\Delta Y$.

Maxwell (1955) too tried to explain the built-in-flexibility of tax system, by relating the tax yield of individual taxes to their respective bases, with which they can be positively correlated. It is believed to be an improvement over Edelberg's method as he tried to relate the tax yield of individual taxes to their respective bases with which, they can be positively correlated. Based upon certain statistical evidence, Maxwell tried to deduce two conclusions. Firstly, he asserts that it seems proper to take National Income or Gross National Product (Y) as the base of measurement of over all built-in-flexibility of the tax system (T) and the resultant equation will be $(\Delta T/\Delta Y).(Y/T)$, where (T) and (Y) are as defined above. Secondly, he maintained that while a particular tax is being considered, it is always plausible to relate changes in tax yield to changes in the precise base upon which tax is levied.

Musgrave (1959) tried to improve the estimate of elasticity by introducing *tax base and tax rate* in the model. Later there were further improvements in the methodology by Wilford (1965), who introduced tax rate as another explanatory variable in the model, in addition to income. Wilford's attempt was to integrate the rate elasticity into the income elasticity with a motive to separate the discretionary changes from the automatic changes in historical tax revenues series. The equation, Wilford had suggested is as follows :

$$\text{Log } T = \log a + b \log Y + c \log r.$$

Where, T = tax revenue, Y = National income, the regression coefficient b gives the percent change in (T), the coefficient a gives the level of revenue r = tax rate and c is the rate of elasticity.

Legler *et al.* (1968) supplemented the same by including employment, income tax and sales tax rates and relative prices of taxed and untaxed goods as explanatory variables. The model suggested by them is a further extension of Wilford's equation stated above. Under the assumption that total tax revenues are derived from income tax and sales tax receipts, the specific formulation advocated by these authors is as follows :

$$\text{Log } T = \log a + b_1 \log Y + c_2 \log N + d_1 \log r_1 + e \log r_2 + f \log P.$$

where, Y = percapita income, N = population r_1 = income tax rate, r_2 = sales tax rate, P = relative price of taxed versus untaxed goods, d = rate elasticity of income tax,e = rate elasticity of sales tax. No doubt, the model is an attempt to study the intricacies of the relationship of ali taxes. The actual operational aspect of the model in an economy with multiple tax system remains elusive.

To overcome the shortcomings of the previous studies, Harris (1968), Singer (1970) and Wasylenko (1975) used the constant structure method to estimate the elasticity and buoyancy of United States personal income taxes. A number economists like Lewis (1962) and Auld (1971) also made use of this method to measure the elasticity and buoyancy o United States' tax structure. Implicit in this method was the questionable assumption that tax payers in all income classes take standard deductions and exemptions. This assumption as Wasylenko argued may result in an overestimate of the effective tax rate and thereby overestimate the elasticity coefficient.

Chaudhary (1975) estimated the elasticity and buoyancy of West Malaysian income tax system, using a Divisia Index Approach. While estimating the elasticity of West Malaysian income tax system, he assumed that there exists the aggregate tax function describing tax yields as a function of K-bases. This function is analogous to a production function showing the aggregate output obtainable from 'n' factors inputs.

In this method of measuring the Buoyancy and Elasticity, Choudhary has considered the continuous differentiable aggregate tax function at each instant of time which he defines :

$$T(t) = f\,[\,X_1(t), \ldots\ X_k\,(t);\,t\,] \ldots\ldots (1)$$

where, T denotes the aggregate tax yield, X1 denotes the proxy tax base for the k categories of taxes and the time variable t is a proxy for discretionary tax measures.

Analogous to the effect of technical changes, the effects of discretionary tax changes at time `t' are obtained by taking the time derivative of `f'. Thus, by taking the logarithm of tax function, differentiating with respect to time (t) and rearranging we get,

$$\frac{ft\,(t)}{f\,(t)} = \frac{T\,(t)}{T\,(t)} - \sum_{1}^{k} \frac{f_i\,(t)\,X_i\,(t)}{f\,(t)} = \frac{X_i\,(t)}{X_i\,(t)} \qquad (2)$$

setting, $\dfrac{f_i\,(t)\,X_i\,(t)}{f\,(t)} = B_i\,(t)$ and,

$$\frac{f_t(t)}{f(t)} = \frac{D(t)}{D(t)}$$

where, D (t) is the Divisia Index of discretionary tax change. Equation (2) can be rewritten as :

$$\frac{D(t)}{D(t)} = \frac{T(t)}{T(t)} - \sum_{l}^{k} B_i(t) \frac{X_i(t)}{X_i(t)} \qquad (3)$$

The apparent shift of the tax function 'f' overtime D(t)/ D_t is the growth of tax revenues owing to discretionary tax measures.

William J. Byrne (1983) estimated the elasticity of the tax system of Zambia for the period 1966-1977. He followed a proportional adjustment method to study the elasticity. The model, he used is as follows :

$$T_{ij} = T_{j-1,j} \quad \frac{T_{j-2,J-1}}{T_{j-1}} \quad \text{——} \quad \frac{T_{2,3}}{T_3} \frac{T_{1,2}}{T_2}$$

Where, T_j denotes the actual tax yield in the 'j'th year. T_{ij} denotes the collection of the 'j'th year adjusted to the structure of the 'i'th year chosen as the reference or base year, and

$$T_{j-1,j} = T_j - D_j$$

where, D_j is the effect (positive or negative) in the 'j'th year of the discretionary change in that year. He derived the estimate of the elasticity by regressing the adjusted tax yield on GNP

Ehtisham Ahmad and Nicholas Stern (1991)[27] estimated the buoyancy of Pakistan's tax structure for the period 1976-77 to 1985-86. They estimated the relation between tax yield and its economic base by using the most conventional method:

$$\log Tt = a + b\log Y_t + E_t$$

Where, T_t is the collection from tax head in question. Y_t is GDP at market price and E_t, a random term which represents the buoyancy. They found that the buoyancy coefficient varied from (1.75) in case surcharges to (0.95) in case of sales tax. Their analysis showed that the surcharges were more buoyant (1.75) in comparison to other taxes. The buoyancy coefficient for sales tax and Excise duty was calculated to be (0.95) and (0.96) respectively.

SECTION-II
STUDIES RELATING TO TAX ELASTICITY AND BUOYANCY IN INDIA

In this section, an attempt has been made to review some of the major studies carried out by various researchers on the estimation of elasticity and buoyancy in India.

The Pioneers in adopting the method of elasticity and buoyancy to measure the tax responsiveness in India are D.T. Lakdawala and Khabadkone (1959). Their work is mainly based upon Bretherton's method. They have discussed in details the methods of eliminating the effects of all other changes not connected with income changes. They have calculated the sensitivity of central taxes by taking into account three sets of tax rates which prevailed during the year 1948-49 and 1954-55 and also a hypothetical tax rate suggested by the Taxation Enquiry Commission. In some cases like union excise duties and custom duties, they have worked out the elasticities by group of commodities taxed.

Sahota (1961) made an attempt to estimate the elasticity of Indian tax system using national income, national expenditure and price level, by taking into consideration the time lag between the changes of income and tax yield. Sahota's analysis of elasticity which he terms as built-in-flexibility and buoyancy which is denoted by him as administrative flexibility pertains to the period 1951-52 to 1957-58. Further, he makes use of the time rate of growth method to measure elasticity of certain taxes which runs in the form of the equation:

$$\frac{\Delta T}{T} / \frac{\Delta I}{I}$$

where, T is the tax yields and (I) is the time period.

Raja.J. Chelliah (1967) undertook an analysis to measure buoyancy of the tax system and its income elasticity. The usual approach adopted is :

$Y = ax^b$, where,

Y = Tax revenue

X = National Income or any other independent variable and `a' and `b' are two parameters.

Rao (1969) attempted to estimate GNP elasticity of tax. Rao's study showed that tax responsiveness to income changes is of the same order: both for the states and the centre, and Jain's study also confirmed the findings of Rao. All these developments enriched the then existing knowledge that indirect taxes are more buoyant than the direct taxes, revealing further, that corporate taxes are the most buoyant, while land revenue, agricultural income-tax and state excise duties were less important as evidenced by income inelasticity.

M. M. Jain (1969) also estimated the income elasticity of the union and the state taxes for the period 1955-56 to 1965-66. His results confirmed the findings of Rao. However, he found that indirect taxes were more buoyant than direct taxes. It means that our additional tax efforts have mostly been confined to indirect taxes. Jain further tried to measure the automatic increase in tax yields which might arise as a result of the interaction between built-in tax structure and changes in GNP. In other words, he found out the response of tax revenues at constant tax formulae to changes in GNP.

Inter-state comparison of tax performance with income elasticity as the sole indicator for some states, specifically, Jammu and Kashmir, West Bengal, Tamil Nadu and Gujarat was carried out by Reddy (1975).

A slightly different approach was adopted by Rao (1979) to study elasticity and buoyancy of state taxes by taking into account factors affecting taxable capacity and tax effort of the states. This was done by segregating the economic factors, political factors and other administrative factors, although, finally the empirical analysis was confined to three economic variables, namely, percentage of income from primary sector, per capita income at constant prices (1971) and working class consumer price indices in the state capital. Further, Rao tried to include two sets of dummy variables, one relating to the political party in power and the other relating to plan period. He calculated the GDP (exclusive of agricultural income) elasticity of tax and elasticity of personal income tax and found that the total GDP elasticity was higher than non-agricultural GDP, and that personal income tax was not elastic.

K.V. Nambiar and M. Govinda Rao (1972) estimated the income elasticity of various taxes to study the tax efforts of different states for the period 1961-62 to1967-68. Their measurement runs as follows:

$$E = \frac{\Delta T}{\Delta T} / \frac{\Delta T}{\Delta Y} = \frac{\Delta T}{T} \cdot \frac{Y}{\Delta Y}$$

Where, E stands for elasticity, ΔT and ΔY for changes in tax revenue and NSDP respectively and T, and Y for tax revenue and NSDP in the base period respectively.

The term income elasticity as used by them runs as the ratio of the percentage change in revenue to the percentage change in NSDP over the period. They called the method as a compact one as the model takes in to account the effects of both the changes in the rate structure and in the base structure on the productivity of taxes.

K.N. Reddy (1975) also calculated the income elasticity of tax revenue to make an inter-state comparison of tax performance. He preferred to derive the Income elasticity of the tax revenue by analyzing the ratio of percentage change in percapita total tax revenue to percentage change in percapita income.

Bagchi and Rao (1982) estimated the elasticity of non-corporate income tax in India for the period 1965-66 to 1978-79, using a log linear model. They tried to regress adjusted tax yield on non-agricultural GDP to arrive at the elasticity figure They have used the model :

$$\text{Log } D_j = \log a + b \log \text{GDP (non-agricultural income)}$$

where, D_j = estimate of adjusted tax yield.

The elasticity for model is `b' which is a constant. Where as elasticity otherwise for a linear model would have been :

$$\eta = \frac{Dj/Dj}{\text{GDP non-agrl./ GDP non-agrl.}}$$

Where, ü is the elasticity, GDP non agrl. is the income originating in the non-agricultural sector, and Dj = estimate of adjusted tax yield.

They further carried out their analysis to study the effects of tax rate change on the total income tax yield for the period 1974-75, 1976-77 and 1977-78. They formulated to alternative models to study the effects of tax rate change on the total yield of income tax :

(i) $B = a + b_1 \text{ GDP} + b_2 D$

(ii) $\text{Log } B = \log a + b_1 \log \text{GDP} + b_2 D$

Where, B = income which would be assessable during the years in question with a uniform exemption limit in the absence of any discretionary change.

D = dummy variable

GDP = Gross Domestic Product at factor cost.

Dass (1987) estimated the Buoyancy and Elasticity of states taxes of Assam for the period 1964-65 to 1978-79. Dass has used the following model to find Buoyancy. He assumed that,

$T_a = \alpha Y^{\beta}$ and, by taking log on the both sides, he has found,

$$\text{Log Ta} = \log \alpha + \beta \log Y,$$

where, he defined β as the buoyancy, Y = state income and T_a = actual tax yield. And, to find the elasticity, he used the same notation, whereas here, the dependent variable is T_c, which is defined as cleaned or hypothetical tax yield. Accordingly, his model comes out to be,

$$\text{Log } T_c = \log \alpha + \eta \log Y,$$

where, η is the elasticity.

The buoyancy analysis for all groups of Assam's taxes showed that, the buoyancy co-efficient was marginally above unity in the cases of each of the state's total taxes (1.063), all direct taxes (1.043), all indirect taxes taken together (1.077), while that of all states taxes was above unity (1.251). Given the usual norm that the buoyancy of taxes should be significantly higher than unity, the over all picture of Assam tax yields appears to be far from satisfactory.

Tax wise analysis showed that purchase tax was more 'buoyant' (co-efficient of buoyancy being 3.406) followed by Taxes and Duties on Electricity and Agricultural Income Tax, with coefficients of 1.576 and 1.385 respectively. On the other hand, state excise duty (0.4151), land revenue (0.066), motor vehicle tax (0.738), though important in the fiscal system, were income in elastic in terms of buoyancy.

Bansal (1988) used the method of regression analysis to estimate buoyancies of tax revenue of all the states, for the period 1967-68 to 1981-82.

The regression equation used was :

$$Y = a\,x^b$$

$$\text{or} \quad \text{Log } Y = \log a + b \log x$$

Where, Y denotes tax revenue

X denotes Net State Domestic Product.

b is the regression coefficient or buoyancy.

The finding of his study can be summarized in the following way.

The buoyancy co-efficient of total revenue for all the states taken together was 1.434, which meant that 1 percent increase in NSDP was accompanied by roughly 1.434 percent increase in total states' revenue. The buoyancy co-efficient for total revenue was more than unity in every states indicating thereby that 1 percent increase in NSDP resulted in more than 1 percent increase in states' total revenue. The buoyancy co-efficient was highest for Himanchal Pradesh (2.099) and the lower for Assam (1.162).

Further the buoyancy co-efficient of states' own total tax revenue for all the states taken together was slightly higher (1.444) than that of total revenue (1.434). The buoyancy co-efficient of states' own total revenues varied from 1.027 for Punjab to 2.745 for Manipur.

By following a similar approach, Amaresh Bagchi and Tapas Sen (1989)[50] estimated the buoyancy of states own tax revenue and sales tax revenue of the 17 states, for the period 1960-61 to 1969-70, 1970-71 to 1979-80 and 1980-81 to 1986-87.

Their estimate shows that the buoyancy co-efficient of states own tax revenue varied from 0.8150 for Assam to 1.6366 in Tamil Nadu for the period 1960-61 to 1969-70. Compare to these years, the buoyancy co-efficient varied from 1.0306 in Bihar to 1.5896 in Andhra Pradesh during the year 1980-81 to 1986-87.

Further, they found that the buoyancy co-efficient of states' sales tax varied from 0.9394 in Bihar to 1.7190 in Andhra Pradesh for the period 1980-81 to 1986-87.

SUMMARY OF THE FINDINGS

Summing up, it may be argued that the elasticity and buoyancy of taxation can be measured by using dummy variables techniques, constant structure method, data adjustment method, and divisia index method. Any choice among these various techniques will no doubt depend upon the data availability and their amenability to various kinds of adjustment. Further, all these three alternative methods suggest that the constant structure methods in general provide more approximate net tax revenues and the data adjustment methods would provide only the second-best approximations as evident from various studies.

Further, all most all the studies have confirmed that while the tax system of developed countries were more buoyant and exhibited a high degree of built-in-flexibility, India's experience in this regard was quite dismal where both the co-efficients of elasticity and buoyancy was invariably less than that of developed countries. Similar variations in tax elasticity and buoyancy were observed in the case of different states in India. On the whole, tax performance of the union and the state Governments was not quite satisfactory. Moreover, within the tax sources, indirect taxes showed to have more elastic and buoyant than that of direct taxes.

Conclusion

The studies reviewed above had made a substantial contribution in identifying some important variables affecting the growth of total tax revenue, interms of its elasticity and buoyancy. But, the influence of the variables indicated by different studies differs markedly across the countries and in country overtime.

It is to be noted that , in the majority of the cases, no

attempt has been made to specify the reasons for a selection of the variables, either on theoretical or statistical grounds. Therefore, an attempt would be made in Chapter-V, to give a comprehensive account of the major conceptual and empirical issues relating to the quantification of income responsiveness (elasticity) as well as total responsiveness (buoyancy) tax system.

NOTES AND REFERENCES

1. Bretherton, R. F.; `The Sensitivity of Taxes To Fluctuations of Trade', in Econometrica, vol. V, 1937, pp. 171-183.
2. Hicks, U.K.,; Finances of British Government : 1920-36, Oxford University Press, London, 1938, Part-II, Chapter -XVIII.
3. Edelberg, V.,; "Flexibility of the Yield of Taxation : Some Econometric Investigation", Journal of the Royal Statistical Society, 1940, Part-II, pp. 153-190.
4. Richard A. Musgrave and Miller,; "Built in Flexibility", American Economic Review, March, 1948, Reprint in Readings in Fiscal Policy, American Economic Association, pp. 379-386.
5. Groves, H.M. and Khan, C.H.,; "The stability of State and Local Tax Yields", American Economic Review, vol. 41, March, 1952, pp. 87-102.
6. Legler, J.B. and Shapiro, P.,; "The Responsiveness of State Tax Revenue to Economic Growth", National Tax Journal, vol. 21 No. 1., March, 1968, p. 47. 7. Richard A. Musgrave., - The Theory of Public Finance, Mc-Graw-Hill Book Co., New York, 1959, pp. 506-507.
8. Joseph A. Pechman.,; Yield of Individual Income Tax During a Recession : Policy to Combet Depression, Princeton University Press, Princeton, 1953, pp. 123-143.
9. Cohen, Leo J.,; "An Empirical Measurement of the Built-in-flexibility of the Individual Income Tax," American Economic Review, Papers and Proceedings, 1959, pp. 532-533.

10. Prest, A.R.,; "The Sensitivity of the Yield of the Personal Income Tax in the United Kingdom", Economic Journal, vol. 72, September, 1962, pp. 576-596.

11. Cohen, Leo J.,; OP. Cit., pp. 532-533.

12. Maxwell, J.A.,; Fiscal Policy, Henry Holt and Co., New York, 1955, pp. 104-115.

13. Wilford, W.T.; "State Tax Stability Criteria and the Revenue Income Elasticity Coefficient Reconsidered", National Tax Journal, vol. 18, No. 3, September, 1965, pp. 304-312.

14. Ray C. L.,; "A Note on State Stability Criteria", National Tax Journal, vol. 19, No. 2, June, 1966, p. 207.

15. Legler, J.B., and Shapiro, P.,; "The Responsive of State Tax Revenue to Economic Growth", National Tax Journal, vol. 21, No. 1, March, 1968, p. 47.

16. Singer, N.M.,; "The use of dummy variables in Estimating the Income Elasticity of State Income Tax Revenues", National Tax Journal, vol. 21, No. 2, June, 1968, pp. 200-204.

17. Hariss, R.,; Income and Sales Taxes : The 1970 Outlook for States and Localities, The Council of State Government, Chicago, 1968, pp. 48-110.

18. Singer, N.M.,; "Estimating State Income Tax Revenues : A New Approach", Review of Economic and Statistics, vol. 52, September, 1970, pp. 427-433.

19. Wasylenko, M.,; "Estimating the Elasticity of State Personal Income Taxes", National Tax Journal, vol. 28, No. 1, March, 1975, p. 140.

20. Lewis, W.Jr.,; Federal Fiscal Policy in the Post war Recessions, D.C. Brookings Institution, Washington, 1962, pp. 29-31.

21. Auld, D.A.L.,; "Automatic Fiscal Stabilizers : Problems of Identification and Measurement", Journal of Public Finance, vol. 26, No. 4, 1971, pp. 513-531.

22. Hariss, R.,; Op. Cit., pp 48-110.

23. Prest, A.R.,; "The Sensitivity of the Yield of the Personal Income Tax in the United Kingdom", Economic Journal, vol. 72, September, 1962, pp. 576-596.

24. Choudhary, Nurun N.,; "A Study of the Elasticity of the West Malaysian Income Tax System", I.M.F. Staff Papers, vol. 22, July, 1975, pp. 494-509.
25. Byrne, William J.,; "The Elasticity of the Tax System of Zambia : 1966-1977", World Development, 1983, vol. II, No. 2, pp. 153-162.
26. Ibid, p. 159. 27. Ahmand, E., and Stern, Nicholas,; The Theory and Practic of Tax Reform in Developing Countries, Cambridge University Press, Cambridge 1991, pp. 45-48.
28. Lakdawala, D.T. and Khambedhone,; "The Sensitivity of Central Taxes : 1948-49 to 1954-55", The Economic Weekly, Dec. 5th and 12th 1959, pp. 1933-1940 and 1675-1681.
29. Sahota, G.S.,; Indian Tax Structure and Economic Development, Asia Publishing House, Bombay, 1961, pp. 12-65.
30. Chelliah, R.J.,; Elasticity and Rate of Growth of State Taxes in Joshi, M.D., (Ed).; Mobilisation of State Revenues, Impex India, New Delhi, 1967, pp. 49-53.
31. Rao, K.B.K.,; "Income Elasticity of Central and States Taxes", Margin, vol. 1, No. 3, April, 1969, pp. 11-21.
32. Jain, M.M.,; "Income Elasticity of Indian Tax Structure 1955-56 to 1965-66", Economic and Political Weekly, vol. IV, No. 18, May 3, 1969, pp. 769-71.
33. Ibid., p. 770.
34. Ibid., p. 771.35. Rao, V.G.,; The Responsiveness of Tax System in India, Allied Publishers Private Limited, New Delhi, 1979.
36. Ibid., pp. 105-107.
37. Ibid., pp. 79-80.
38. Ibid., p. 80.
39. Nambiar, K.V. and Rao, M. Govinda,; "Tax Performance of States", Economic and Political Weekly, vol. VII, No. 21, May 20, 1972, p. 1036.
40. Reddy, K.N.,; "Inter State Tax Effort", Economic and Political Weekly, vol. X, No. 50, December 13, 1975, pp. 1961-1967.
41. Rao, M. Govinda.,; "Economic and Political Determinants of

States Tax Revenue and Political Weekly, vol. XIV, No. 47, November 24, 1979, p. 1925.

42. Ibid., p. 1922.
43. Ibid., p. 1925.
44. Ibid., p. 1932.
45. Bagchi, Amaresh and Rao, Govinda.,; "Elasticity of Non-corporate Income Tax in India", Economic and Political Weekly, September 4, 1982, pp. 1452-1458.
46. Ibid., p. 1458.
47. Dass, S.K.,; Dynamics of Taxation in a Developing Economy: With Special Reference to Assam, Omsons Publications, Guwahati, 1987, pp. 132-174.
48. Ibid., p. 137.
49. Bansal, R.K.,; Raising Additional Resources in the States, Atlantic Publishers and Distributors, New Delhi, 1988, pp. 47-50.
50. Bagchi, A. and Sen, T.,; Kerala's Revenue Potential : projections for 1990-95, National Institute New Delhi, 1989, pp. 1-14.

CHAPTER - III

METHODOLOGY

INTRODUCTION

An analysis of the compositional pattern of Orissa's tax revenues in the preceding chapter showed that, on its own resource mobilization front, Orissa failed to attain a desirable level of financial self-reliance in general and, that with respect to its own taxing power in particular, its performance was not satisfactory. As a result of which, the financial dependence of the state on the union Government has been on the increase in recent years. Further, our analysis carried out so far suggests that, Orissa made half-hearted tax efforts during the period under study, as a matter of which the observed anamolies in the state's tax system has been the resultant outcome in recent years.

THRUST OF THE PROBLEM

All these observed trends noted above provide a solid ground for the necessity and the desirability of undertaking an analysis of the efficiency of the state tax measures. Accordingly, we have made an attempt in this chapter to review the responsiveness and productivity of Orissa's tax system in terms of the indicators noted in section 1.2 of chapter I, i.e. in terms of elasticity and buoyancy, to measure the relative degree of efficiency of the state tax measures on the one hand, and to indicate the extent of additional tax efforts needed to increase the revenue of the Government on the other hand. This besides being essential for arriving at a proper assessment of the overall success of the state Government's measure to increase tax revenue would enable us to ascertain, how the revenue potential of a given tax system has been realized. So, the related questions that we will touch upon in this context are :

(i) Whether the state of Orissa has succeeded in evolving a tax structure characterised by strong built-in-responsiveness of tax revenue with respect to state income growth? If, it is so, to what extent? If it is not then to what extent, it has relied excessively on discretionary changes to improve tax yields and,

(ii) Which of the individual tax items of the state are responsible for the inelasticity of Orissa's tax structure and to what extent, the inelasticity of Orissa's tax structure is responsible for its excessive dependence on the centre.

This chapter, which is the core of our study, is divided into three parts. In section-I, an outline of the concepts and the method of estimating buoyancy and elasticity employed in this study are presented. Noting the difficulties associated with the estimation of elasticity and buoyancy of the tax system, an attempt is made to develop an alternative model of elasticity and buoyancy for measuring the responsiveness of Orissa's tax system in order to arrive at the answers to the questions posed above. An estimation of elasticity and buoyancy of the state tax system as a whole is carried out in section-II and, in section-III, we present an analysis of elasticity and buoyancy of individual state's taxes.

SECTION - I (METHODOLOGY)

BUOYANCY AND ELASTICITY : CONCEPTS

On the state level, the growth in tax revenue may come about through `automatic' response of the tax yields to changes in Net State Domestic Product (NSDP) and/or, through the imposition of new taxes, revision of the rate structure of existing taxes, expansion of the tax base, making tax compliance harder by law and other administrative measures backed by legal action.

Changes in tax yield resulting from modifying tax parameters (i.e. rate, base, etc.) are called `discretionary changes'. They are the result of legislative action. With tax parameters held constant (i.e. discretionary) changes being eliminated), automatic changes in tax yield resulting from variations in NSDP measures the elasticity of a tax system. However changes in the tax yield flowing from the combined effect of 'automatic' changes and 'discretionary' changes are a measure of the 'buoyancy' of a tax or a tax system.

An analysis of such buoyancy and elasticity is important for many reasons. First, to the extent that the buoyancy is low, it would suggest a need for devising a tax structure which would overcome the deficiencies. Secondly, on the basis of such study, a state Government can estimate the probable tax revenue with unchanged base and rate of tax consequent upon mere increase in the NSDP. Thirdly, it would be helpful in indicating the extent of additional tax effort needed to increase the revenue of the Government.

HISTORICAL APPROACH TO THE MEASURE OF ELASTICITY AND BUOYANCY

In the case of understanding the tax responsiveness in the frame-work of methodology, there is a distinct dichotomy, one is referred to as tax buoyancy and the other is tax elasticity (as noted earlier). Even though, the total tax receipts are influenced by both National/State income and tax base, yet, the synergic effect of each of the pertinent influences variable remains to be seen in isolation. The composite nature of behaviour of the tax format sometimes creates problems for tax analysts since base and income are correlated phenomena. Rao (1978)[1] has remarked that, "the coefficient obtainable by relating the changes in the net tax yields to those in National income is termed as built-in-flexibility or elasticity measure of the tax system". Where as, "the coefficient obtainable by relating the changes in the historical tax receipts to changes in National income is tax buoyancy". Thus, one relates to the partial account of tax responsiveness to changes in National income (in our study, we will refer it as state income) and, the other is related to total responsiveness. If, this theory holds true, then the problem is to be viewed, how the total responsiveness would in isolation, in changes in state income or vice-versa would react to the total tax yields. The marginal tax rate, while defined as the ratio of absolute changes in tax revenue to the absolute changes in the National/State income, which, when considered as a ratio of percentage change in National/State income gives as income elasticity. It is statistically established that,

$$T = f(B) \qquad (1)$$

$$\text{and, } T = f(B, Y) \qquad (2)$$

Where, T = Tax revenue

B = Base

and, Y = National or state income.

Given, these two equations, it can be shown that,

$$E_{TB} = \frac{\Delta T / T}{\Delta B / B} \qquad (3)$$

$$E_{YB} = \frac{\Delta B / B}{\Delta Y / Y} \qquad (4)$$

Where, equation (3) refers to Rate response, i.e.;the response of the tax to its base (ETB) and, equation (4) refers to base response, i.e.; the response of the tax base to state income (EYB). From equation (3) and (4), it may be derived that,

$$E_{TY} = \left(\frac{\Delta T/T}{\Delta B/B}\right) \cdot \left(\frac{\Delta B/B}{\Delta Y/Y}\right)$$

$$= \left(\frac{\Delta T/T}{\Delta Y/Y}\right) \qquad \text{———— (5)}$$

Where, E_{TY} = Elasticity of tax with respect to state income.

The above equation states that the response of a tax is a product of its response to base and the response of that base to the state income. With these definitions in mind, it was attempted to show that, the overall response of a tax system may be calculated as the weighted sum of individual tax's income elasticities, the weights being the proportions of individual taxes in total tax revenue. But soon we would realize that the equation (4) can be directly obtained as a single regression coefficient, if, we adopt a multiplicative type of model, i.e.

$$\text{Log } T = a_0 + a_1 \text{ Log } B + a_2 \text{ Log } Y + U \qquad \text{———— (6)}$$

where, B = Tax Base

Y = State income

ai = Parameters of the variables (i=0,1,2) and, U = Disturbance term.

The ordinary least square estimation of the parameters ai will not be valid unless the following assumptions are fulfilled regarding the disturbance term. As for example,

$E(U) = 0$ ———— (i)

$E(Ui^2) = 6^2$, a constant ———— (ii)

$E(U_iU_j) = 0$, for $i \neq j$ ———— (iii)

According to assumption (iii) that, there is no autocorrelation in the disturbance term. But, often it is found in practice (Bez, 1990)[2], that in the time series analysis, there is always autocorrelation present. This is due to the upheavals in the economy. As a result, errors are not always the same. Sometimes, it is increasing and sometimes, they are decreasing.

In equation (6), $a_2 = E_{TY}$, since, logarithmic equation yields coefficients, which are themselves elasticities of the respective concomitant variables. It can be shown mathematically as follows :

$$T = a_0 B^{a1} Y^{a2} \quad \text{——— (a)}$$

$$\frac{\delta T}{\delta B} = a_0 a_1 B^{a1-1} Y^{a2} \quad \text{——— (b)}$$

$$\frac{\delta T}{\delta B} = a_0 a_2 B^{a1} Y^{a2-1} \quad \text{——— (c)}$$

$$E_{TB} = \frac{\Delta T / T}{\Delta B / B} = \frac{\Delta T}{\Delta B} \cdot \frac{B}{T} = \frac{a_0 a_1 B^{a1-1} Y^{a2} . B}{a_0 B^{a1} Y^{a2}} \quad \text{——— (d)}$$

Where, a_l = constant ——— (e)

T = Total tax realized

B = Base

Y = State income

a_i = the coefficient of the equation

and, ETB = elasticity

It is a different matter, whether we would like to have constant elasticity or variable elasticity. If, we go for variable elasticity, i.e.; time point elasticity, then the equation (5) will be of use. What actually we need to investigate into, is the effect of base in isolation of state income to total tax receipts. It is found in practice that, Base could be eliminated from the system of equation. Instead of taking base as an independent variable, we thought it practicable, to introduce another variable which may be termed as discretionary effort of tax tilizing n and, will act as a substitute for this variable, i.e.; Base. We must note it here that discretionary measures not only include legislated change in the tax base but also, (a) changes in tax rates, (b) the multiplication of levies, (c) the extension of taxation to areas hither to not covered by the tax, (d) the conversion of specific taxes into advalorem taxes, (e) the substitution of a single-point tax by a double or multi-point one, (f) the withdrawal of or reduction in exemptions, rebates or tax holidays, and so on. Further, it must be noted here that, all these discretionary changes noted above relates directly to the tax base. Almost, it is an established fact that - if, from the total tax, that part of tax realization accounted for discretionary efforts is substracted, then the net tax yields will have a direct linear or loglinear functional relationship with state income in order to find the elasticities later on. If, we examine thoroughly, the two statistical variables as two distinct variables as base and the discretionary effort, then, what we must find that, their covariance is so strong that, it will yield pearson coefficient (r) almost equal to one. Only, in such a situation, base could be a substitute for discretionary effort, which can be shown mathematically as follows,

$$\text{Cov (B, D)} \neq 0$$

$$\text{and, } r = \frac{Cov(B,D)}{\sqrt{V(B)V(D)}} = 1$$

Where, B = Base, and D = Discretionary measures.

Only then, in a regression equation, both B and D, if included as independent variables, the problem of multicollinearity would arise and the estimates of regression coefficient become in-estimable. If, the above proposition holds true, then, why could we not take another version of, T = f(D,Y), where, both D and Y are related to T, because we may also take tax as a function of state income alone, thus,

$$\text{Log } T = a_0 + a_1 \log Y + U \quad \text{———} \quad (7)$$

Where, T = Tax realized

Y = State income

U = Disturbance term, which is assumed to be normally distributed with zero mean and unit variance and,

a_i = parameters of the variables

(i = 0, 1)

The above equation would also give us ETY. From this equation, neither we need to consider the individual taxes separately within the total tax receipts, because such a task will lead to statistical complicacy, nor, we can find logic in adopting a seemingly uncompromising methodology to assess ETY as a product of marginal tax and income elasticity of individual tax, defined as (Rao, 1978)3,

$$E_{ty} = \Sigma t/T.\, E_{ty} \quad \text{———} \quad (8)$$

where, E_{TY} = Income response of individual tax,

T = Aggregate Tax Revenue

t = Revenue from a particular tax

and, Y = National/State income.

Since, both base and income effects total tax revenue and with dominant periodic effect, therefore, to study the tax system over a longer period, the appropriate methodology would be to adopt a model, which is statistically viable.

It is difficult to ascertain, which model will be statistically satisfactory, when there involved probable multiple interpretation of tax theory. We present here some of the models that have been used (Rao, 1979)4.

$$\text{Log } T = \log a_1 + b_1 \log B \quad \text{———} \quad (9)$$

$$\text{Log } B = \log a_2 + b_2 \log Y \quad \text{———} \quad (10)$$

Where, T = Total tax revenue

B = Tax base

Y = National/state income.

A_1 and a_2 = constant terms and,

b_1 and b_2 = regression coefficient of B and Y respectively.

There appears some other econometric impropities, the equation (9) as such possess no problem and also it is in accordance with the theory of taxation. But, the equation (10) would certainly be superfluous and if not statistically violative. Since, equation (9) and (10) implied that Base is functionally related to income, which in turn is related to tax. In the presence of probable multicollinearity, why can't we use tax as a function of both Base and Income? Because, the method that, Rao has suggested would not yield estimate of the parameters for a simple reason that the number of equations is less than the number of parameters to be estimated. Therefore, we are having a safe way to define tax yield as,

$$T = f(Y, B) \qquad (11)$$

In the above equation, the exogeneous variables Y and B are assumed to be independent. If, they are correlated, that is functionally represented as,

$$B = f(Y) \qquad (12)$$

then, the resulting variance-covariance matrix produced by equation (10) would have serious multicollinearity problem, which we would like to avoid. However, Rao has treated both (9) and (10) as a set of simultaneous equations. In that case, the problem of identification arises. As, we see, the transplantation of equation (10) into equation (9) does not yield anything because it remains under identified, since the number of parameters to be estimated from,

$$\text{Log } T = \log a_1 + b_1 \log a_2 + b_1b_2 \log Y \qquad (13)$$

is more than the number of parameters estimated from

equation (13). Hence, it is a futile exercise.

Yet, there is another model (Wilford, 1965)[5].

$$\text{Log } T = \log a + b \log Y + c \log r \quad \text{———} \quad (14)$$

This also leads us to statistical problem. If, r happens to be the tax rate defined in terms of total tax revenue over the units of time, then, logically, we donot find anything new as regards to estimate the tax responsiveness to changes in income. This view is also supported by Wilford. The equation (14) is remodelled as,

$$\text{Log } T = \log a + b \log Y + c \log r + d \log B \quad \text{———} \quad (15)$$

where, all the variables are defined earlier (Ray, 1966)6. In order to relate r with T, or, for estimating T, we can use a very simple model,

$$T = T_0 e^r \quad \text{———} \quad (16)$$

where, T_0 = Tax revenue at the base period

and r = Rate of the tax.

But, our problem is to find buoyancy and elasticity and if, possible to isolate them. Some other authors even go a step further to modify equation (14) and equation (15) as (Legler et al, 1968)9,

$$\text{Log } T = \log a + b \log \hat{Y} + C \log N + d \log r_1 + e \log r_2 + f \log P \quad \text{———} (17)$$

where, $\hat{Y}$ = percapita income

N = population

r_1 = income tax rate

r_2 = sales tax rate

and, P =relative price of taxed versus untaxed goods.

First, it is a composite equation for determining all taxes, whether it is ethical to do so or not is another matter for examination. Still, there is another statistical irregularity which the author seems to ignore. The exogeneous variable

N and $\hat{Y}$ are correlated, i.e. covariance (N, $\hat{Y}$) $\neq 0$, since, while estimating the percapita income the N variable is utilized, hence the same variable cannot appear another time in disguise. The authors only lament for its infeasibility for application, since tax system is not that uniform.

The alternative method is suggested with the model,

$$\text{Log AT} = \log a + b \log Y \quad \text{——————} \quad (18)$$

Where, AT = adjusted tax revenue

Finally, the empirical analysis, was vested with,

$$\text{Log AT} = \log a_1 + b_1 \log Y + U \quad \text{——————} \quad (19)$$

$$\text{Log T} = \log a_2 + b_2 \log Y + V \quad \text{——————} \quad (20)$$

Where, T = historical tax yields.

To estimate the built-in-flexibility and buoyancy for the specified tax groups and individual taxes.

All these theoretical models, are product of tax logistics. Every model is mathematically true. But, empirically, they might not be sound enough. Since, we know, that, tax could be considered as a product of r and B, where r is the rate of tax and, B is the base. While, we are tilizing B as an independent variable in estimating tax, then r should automatically appear as another independent variable with only one restriction that such model be always multiplicative. So, why do not we try a model of this nature which is not indifferent to the existing tax theories? If, we define;

$$T = f(B,r) \quad \text{——————} \quad (21)$$

where, T = Total tax

B = Tax base

and, r = Tax rate

In which case, the model will be :

$$T = \alpha_0 B^{\alpha 1} r^{\alpha 2} \quad \text{——————} \quad (22)$$

where, a1 and a2 = coefficient of B and r.

with the restriction that, $\alpha_1 + \alpha_2 \leq 1$.

Also, we may suggest another model, i.e., a simple variation of the above,

$$r = f\left(\frac{T}{B}\right)$$

$$= \alpha_0 T^{\alpha 1} B^{-\alpha 2} \qquad \text{———————} \qquad (23)$$

Where , r = tax rate.

These two simple models utilize both base and rate of tax as independent variables.

Looking at these models, we found that, tax yield may not be a function of just one variable, i.e. state income, but, number of other independent variables. Therefore, we decide to use tax yield as,

$$T = f(D, Y) \qquad \text{———————} \qquad (24)$$

where, D = Discretionary effects and,

Y = state income

There are advantages and disadvantages in two variable models. Definitely, in a multivariate model, the coefficient of Determination (R^2) is higher, whereas, in a two variable model, R^2 is often smaller as the effects of other variables are ignored. On the other hand, in the estimate of the parameters of regression equations in a multivariate model, their empirical values are distributed in such a way, that the estimate relating to the principal variable becomes smaller. Therefore, equation (17), we considered to be a weak equation.

SECTION III

THE PRESENT APPROACH TO MEASURE ELASTICITY AND BUOYANCY

Keeping in view the infeasibilities of the existing models to the heterogeneous tax structure, we have made a humble attempt in this chapter, to develop our own model. We have adopted a method which we call it as Econometric Approach.

ECONOMETRIC APPROACH

To measure elasticity, we have to separate the effects of changes in tax revenue with respect to "Base". When, T is related to "Income" as well as "Base", the multiple regression model suggested by the empirical analysis in the literature,

$$\text{Log } T = a_1 + a_2 \log Y + a_3 \log B + U \quad \text{———} \quad (25)$$

where, T = Total tax yield,

Y = state income

B = Tax Base, U = disturbance term and,

a_i = estimates of the parameters $(i = 0,1,2)$

does give the account of tax estimation, where the other variables like tax rate and its growth etc. are not incorporated into the model. On this ground, we thought it imperative to substitute the variable D (as defined earlier) for B, where D includes all sorts of discretionary changes. If, we will have to believe that estimate of tax be separable as automatic response (elasticity) and discretionary response, then, the combination of these two responses, will give us the buoyancy of a tax or that of the tax system as a whole. Then,

$$T = T_D + T_Y \quad \text{———} \quad (26)$$

where, T_D = Response of the tax to discretionary changes (B)

T_Y = Automatic response of the tax to changes in income (Y)

and, T = Total unadjusted tax yields from theses two effects.

So, from the total response of the tax (T), we will have to separate the effects' of income and the effects of discretionary changes (base). But, this is not an easy task unless, we know the marginal probability distribution of tax with respect to both automatic as well as discretionary changes.

Since, in the equation (25), the discretionary response and automatic response of the tax are given by the estimates of a3 and a2 (being a log-linear model) and these are constant throughout the period under study, it would be mathematically possible to estimate that part of tax revenue which will be accounted only by automatic response (Income) or discretionary response (Base), e.g., the empirical equation:

$$\text{Log } \hat{T} = \hat{a}_1 + \hat{a}_2 \log Y + \hat{a}_3 \log D \quad \text{———} \quad (27)$$

from which, after taking anti-log, we can get the adjusted tax revenue series as

$$T - \theta_1 T \approx Ta \quad \text{———} \quad (28)$$

where, $\theta_1 T = \hat{a}_3 \log D$ (i.e. the response of the tax to the discretionary measures).

Then, we can re-estimate,

$$Ta = a_4 + a_5 \log Y \quad \text{———} \quad (29)$$

The above equation (29) will give us the elasticity. In this process, we eliminated the effect of discretionary changes from the original multiple regression. The same procedures could be used also for eliminating the effect of income from the tax by subtracting from,

$$T - \theta_2 T = T_D \quad \text{———} \quad (30)$$

where, T_D =Response of the tax due to discretionary measures.

The theoretical considerations though appear to be sound, but due to the presence of constant (intercept), when both Discretionary and income variables act as independent variables then, this constant term of the empirical equation may be partly influenced by income and partly by the discretionary variable in an indirect way, or, it may be free from their effect. According to empiricists, tax could only be a function of both Y and D, or, Y and D separately. That means, the contribution of Y and D, both separately and as well as jointly can be seen from the model structure. But, then the constant term α_0-how could we explain! Therefore, we may suggest a regression equation, which is going through the mean value of the variables, then, we can avoid the problem of α_0. For example,

$$\log(T - \overline{T}) = \hat{\alpha}_1 \log(Y - \overline{Y}) + \hat{\alpha}_2 \log(D - \overline{D}) \text{——— } (30.1)$$

Where, $\overline{T}, \overline{Y}, \overline{D}$ are the mean values of T, Y, and D respectively.

We may also think that $\hat{\alpha}_0$ is free from the effect of both Y and D. This contribution to the tax given by the value of $\hat{\alpha}_0$ are those functions such as additional tax efforts, new means adopted for resource mobilisation etc., which are always inherent in the tax structure. That is why, when we are estimating T relating to Y or, T relating to D alone we used,

$$T = \theta_1 T - (D) \text{ ——— } (31)$$

$$T = \theta_2 T - (Y) \text{ ——— } (32)$$

Where, $\theta_1 = \hat{a}_3 \log D$, and, $\theta_2 = \hat{a}_4 \log Y$.

Therefore, we have to make an alternative way of removing the effect of either the discretionary factor or the income factor. For example, we take,

$$\text{Log } T = a_6 + a_7 \log Y + U \text{ ——— } (33)$$

Here, the assumption is that the total tax is explained by income alone. The empirical equation,

$$\text{Log } \hat{T} = \hat{a}_6 + \hat{a}_7 \text{Log } Y \text{ ——— } (34)$$

gives the estimate of tax as a function of income. Here, the intercept term gives the account of that element of tax which is beyond the ambit of the model, say, extraneous causes, but certainly not by income variable. We estimate,

$$T_d = T - Ty \text{ ——— } (35)$$

$$\text{Now, } Ty \approx \theta_3 \approx a_6 \log Y \text{ ——— } (36)$$

if, our assumptions are correct then, we re-estimate,

$$Td = \hat{a}_8 + \hat{a}_9 \log D \text{ ——— } (37)$$

Though, $\hat{a}_8$ still present in the model, this is bound to be smaller than $\hat{a}_{10}$ of,

$$\text{Log } \hat{T} = \hat{a}_{10} + \hat{a}_{11} \log D \quad \text{———} \quad (38)$$

This is not only probability, but, the empirical evidence will support the view.

We have to consider one fact that in the previous chapters, we have been discussing the variations of tax realizations in different years, which have to be also supported by empirical evidence within the model. For this reason, we may suggest a linear equation as against the log linear equation. In a multiplicative type of the model, the total effect of any change does not conform to the theory of additivity. For example,

$$Y = a + bx \quad \text{———} \quad (39)$$

$$\text{and, } \text{Log } Y = \log a + b \log x \quad \text{———} \quad (40)$$

where, Y denotes tax revenue

x denotes Net State Domestic Product

and, b denotes regression coefficient.

Here, a + b of the equation (39) = 1. But, in the log linear equation, represented by equation (40), $a + b \neq 1$. For the simple reason, to explain the variation of tax for every single year, we would prefer a linear equation, which supports the additivity property of the parameters estimates.

Next, we have to consider another theoretical constraint. The authorities investigating the buoyancy and elasticity of tax revenue have adopted with solid grounding that,

$$T = f_1 (Y)$$

$$T = f_2 (D) \quad \text{———} \quad (41)$$

$$D = f_3 (Y)$$

This would lead us to the problem of multicollinearity. In that case, the model will be,

$$\text{Log } T = a + b \log Y + c \log B + U \quad \text{———} \quad (42)$$

This is inconsistent and untenable econometrically.

Therefore, we have to make a compromise by adopting only the 2-variables model suggested by these functions.

Further, we know that we rely on the independent Variables to such an extent that at least 50 percent of the total variability could be explained. The coefficient of determination (R^2) will tell us this. But, often from practice, we find that any addition of independent variables will contribute to R^2 but at the cost of reliability of the estimates of the parameters. Also, in time series type of analysis, the disturbance term `U' does not behave in the way we expect, as often, there is serial correlation of the disturbance term. If, we consider the 1st order auto-regression function of the disturbance term, then, we can express,

$$U_t = \rho U_{t-1} + V_t \quad \text{——— (43)}$$

and, the estimate of can be obtained by :

$$\hat{\rho} = \frac{\Sigma \hat{U}_t \hat{U}_{t-1}}{\Sigma U_{t-1}^2} \quad \text{——— (44)}$$

Keeping this in mind, that ρ is also affecting the reliability of the estimate, we re-introduce the earlier model as such,

$$\text{Log } T_t = a_{1t} + a_{2t} \log Y_t + a_{3t} \log D_t + U_t \quad \text{———(45)}$$

and, with one period log,

$$\text{Log } T_{t-1} = a_{1t-1} + a_{2t-1} \log Y_{t-1} + a_{3t-1} \log D_{t-1} + U_{t-1} \text{ ——— (46)}$$

Multiplying the lagged equation by throughout and subtracting from the (45), we obtain,

$$(\text{Log } T_t - \hat{\rho}\, T_t) = (a_{1t} - \hat{\rho}\, a_{1t-1}) + (a_{2t} - \hat{\rho}\, a_{2t-1})$$

$$(\log Y_t - \rho\, Y_{t-1}) + (a_{3t} - \ a_{3t-1})$$

$$(\log B_t - \ D_{t-1}) + (U_t - \ U_{t-1}) \text{ ———(47)}$$

if, we express the above equation (47) as,

$$\text{Log } Tt^* = a_{1t}^* + a_{2t}^* \log Yt^* + a_{3t}^* \log D_t^* + V_t^* \text{ ——(48)}$$

Then,this Vt* will have to hold the same properties as the Ut.

If, we now follow the same procedure in isolating "income" or "discretionary" effect, then we can estimate the automatic response and the discretionary response that constitute the total tax revenue.

In conclusion, for our analysis, we may adopt the following models.

$$T = a_0 + a_1Y + U_1 \qquad (49)$$

$$TA = a_2 + a_3Y + U_2 \qquad (50)$$

$$T = a_4 + a_5Y + a_6D + U_3 \qquad (51)$$

where, T = Actual tax revenue realized

TA = Adjusted tax revenue after taking out discretionary effects.

D = Discretionary effort of tax realization.

U_i = Stochastic disturbance term.

and, Y = state income.

Equation (49) measures the buoyancy of tax revenue, whereas equation (50) measures the elasticity of tax revenue we may also adopt log linear version of the above models. Equation (51) measures the total responsiveness of the tax or the tax system, which is decomposed into two effects namely income response and discretionary response.

In empirical analysis, we shall use the methods mentioned here to separate the effects of discretionary changes to measure the elasticity.

PROBABILISTIC APPROACH

The alternative method that we suggest runs in terms of probabilistic procedure as mentioned earlier.

This is based on the theory of probability and the model is derived by Bez (1990)[8], known as Bez Reaction function. Before, proceeding with the mathematical exposition of the pre-conditions lay down in support of this model.

(i) The model may be treated as the sophisticated type of probability distribution-marginal.

(ii) It is assumed that, when there are two things say object and agent then, the resultant reaction is no more as regards to the effects produced by them and there is no room for externalities.

(iii) It has wide range of application due to the adhoc nature of the model. The model has been applied so for (a) to isolate the effect of use of fertilizers and Man-hours employed to produce yields of certain crops (b) to find, whether the production variation of agricultural output in the seven states of North-East India is to be accredited to spatial or time factors.

(iv) the main stem of analysis is graphical because assuming that the respective objects or agents would behave rather in a rational way.

The model is conceived as, the details of which can be found elsewhere (Bez, 1990)[10].

We are using the symbols familiar to our own type of analysis. The reaction function is giving as,

$$T_{ij} = F_{ij}\,(Y_i,\, D_j) \qquad \text{———————} \qquad (52)$$

From this, we can derive the probability distribution function as,

$$\rho\,(T_{ij}/Y_i,\, D_j) = \rho\,(T_{11}/Y_1,\, D_1) + \ldots. + \rho\,(T_{1n}/Y_1,\, D_j)$$
$$+ \rho\,(T_{21}/Y_2,\, D_1) + \ldots. + \rho\,(T_{2n}/Y_2,\, D_j)$$
$$+\ldots..+ \rho\,(T_{n1}/Y_i,\, D_1) +\ldots.+ \rho\,(T_{nm}/Y_i,\, D_j) \qquad \text{————} (53)$$

Let us consider the observed matrix Tij.

Finally, summing up all the probable functions n, we get the composite function which we can write,

$$P\,(T_{ij}/Y_iD_j) = f\,(Y_i,D_j) \qquad \text{————————} (54)$$

D_j

		D_1	D_2	D_3	D_n
	Y_1	T_{11}	T_{12}	T_{13}	T_{1n}
	Y_2	T_{21}	T_{22}	T_{23}	T_{2n}
Y_i		$\downarrow$			
	$\downarrow$		$((T_{ji}))$		
	Y_n	T_{n1}	T_{n2}	T_{n3}........	T_{nm}

In any sub-set of tax revenues, we may have, say 2 types of responses,

$$P\ (t^m/T_1), \text{ and, } P\ (t^q/T_1) \qquad \text{———(55)}$$

These can be expressed independently,

$$P\ (t^m/T_1, D_j) = \frac{P\ (t^m/T_1)}{P\ (T_1/T)} \qquad \text{———(56)}$$

$$P\ (t^q/T_1, Dj) = \frac{P\ (t^2/T_1)}{P\ (T_1/T)} \qquad \text{———(57)}$$

or, we may possibly get a probability function of the following type.

$$P\,(t^m/T_1) + P\,(t^q/T_1) \qquad (58)$$

$$\text{and, } \Sigma P(t^{m+q}/T_1) = P(T_1/T) \qquad (59)$$

Similarly, for each sub-set, we can imagine the same type of distribution function.

Finally, the model is made operational, by taking the logistic function of the type,

$$\text{Log } Y_j = a + b \log Y_j + U_1 \qquad (60)$$

$$\text{and, Log } D_{i}. = \alpha + \beta \log di. + U_2 \qquad (61)$$

i.e., for each income variant and the discretionary variant, there will yield as many regression lines as there are number of incomes and discretionary measures. Hence, the time series type of analysis, we can say that the same tax revenue series will have a line with the tangents supposed to be all proportionally equal if the income as well as discretionary variable behave rationally. However, with this type of analysis, unlike the econometric analysis, we cannot see straight way, the quantum of tax revenue as income responsive or discretionary measure responsive, since probability function deals even minute variation.

Since, we donot have data according to the choice of this probabilistic model, we rather confine ourselves to econometric type of analysis.

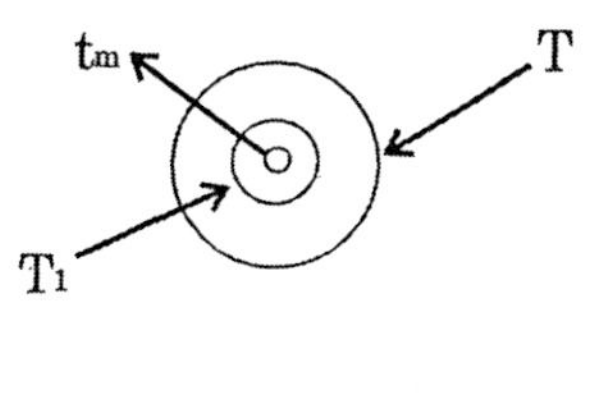

Conceptual illustration

CHAPTER - IV

TAX-EXPENDITURE POLICIES IN ORISSA

INTRODUCTION

This chapter is concerned with an analytical and critical evaluation of the tax-expenditure policies of Orissa, during the period 1961-62 to 1993-94. Such an analysis is carried out in terms of the trends and patterns of the State's tax revenue and Public expenditure. The purpose of this chapter is to study, what were the overall trends in state's tax revenue and public expenditures in the last thirty three years of planning and further to study, what were the directions of change in the Government's tax-expenditure policies. Ultimately, it is the size and composition of taxation and public expenditures that the community looks to. But, under the policy controversies that always surfaces in a growing economy, vital questions about the actual behaviour of these taxation and public expenditures need composed analysis. This is what has been set out in this chapter.

An attempt has been made to review the trends and pattern of the public revenues and public expenditures of the state in relation to some of the important economic variables. This, it is thought would provide some of the necessary overall background and analysis useful for a better understanding and evaluation of the structure and composition of tax revenue and public expenditures, that the study intends to carry out in the next chapter.

ANALYSIS OF REVENUE ACCOUNT

Table 4.1 presents the important relationship between the revenue receipts and revenue expenditures of the Orissa state Government for over three decades from 1961-62 to 1993-94.

The trend of total revenue receipts of the State since 1961-62 is revealed in Column 1. Revenue receipts show a rising trend in absolute term throughout the period from 1961-62 to 1993-94, increasing from Rs. 46.13 crores in 1961-62 to Rs. 3444.4 crores in 1993-94. The annual rate of increase on an average works out to be of 223.23 percent. This increase can be attributed to the rising share of all the sectors in the state domestic product, resultant increase in tax bases and the growth of tax rates over the years and finally due to a larger devolution of resources from the centre to the state by way of higher share in the central taxes

Column 2, shows the state's revenue expenditures for the three decades. The revenue expenditures which were at Rs. 61.35 crores in the year 1961-62, increased to Rs. 3626.0 crores in the year 1993-94, exhibiting an average annual rate of increase of 176.07 percent. This increase of the state's revenue expenditures over the years was mainly due to massive and huge expenditures that the government has carried out to build up its social over head capital to satisfy the growing social and economic needs of a masses who struggle for a reasonable minimal standard of living in the face of acute poverty and unemployment.

It was thought imperative to calculate the exponential growth rates of the revenue receipts and revenue expenditures. For estimating the growth rate, the formula used in both cases, is:

$$Y = ae^{rt}$$

Where, t = time,

Y = revenue receipts or revenue expenditures as the case may be,

r = growth rate.

TABLE 4.1

REVENUE RECEIPTS AND EXPENDITURES OF THE GOVERNMENT OF ORISSA, 1961-62 TO 1993-94.

(Rs. in crores)

YEAR	REVENUE RECEIPTS	REVENUE EXPENDITURES	SURPLUS (+)/ DEFICIT (-)
0	1	2	3
1961-62	46.13	61.35	(-) 15.21
1962-63	62.27	65.99	(-) 3.72
1963-64	69.29	72.01	(-) 2.72
1964-65	74.98	79.20	(-) 4.23
1965-66	80.39	91.31	(-) 10.92
1966-67	106.80	104.42	(+) 2.38
1967-68	109.03	113.20	(-) 4.17
1968-69	116.62	131.77	(-) 15.15
1969-70	131.13	131.01	(+) 0.12
1970-71	135.83	139.89	(-) 4.06
1971-72	151.32	175.08	(-) 23.76
1972-73	168.14	192.78	(-) 24.64
1973-74	174.62	212.46	(-) 37.84
1974-75	227.37	223.51	(+) 3.86
1975-76	277.46	276.18	(+) 1.28
1976-77	305.90	288.30	(+) 17.60
1977-78	346.80	319.00	(+) 27.80
1978-79	423.10	378.00	(+) 45.10
1979-80	467.60	448.90	(+) 18.70

(Condt..)

0	1	2	3
1980-81	621.30	540.50	(+) 80.80
1981-82	601.50	573.60	(+) 27.90
1982-83	801.60	824.60	(-) 23.00
1983-84	783.10	782.70	(+) 0.40
1984-85	823.50	897.20	(-) 73.70
1985-86	940.80	1000.90	(-) 60.10
1986-87	1228.20	1247.90	(-) 19.70
1987-88	1333.10	1407.60	(-) 74.50
1988-89	1550.90	1658.70	(-) 107.80
1989-90	1740.70	1846.10	(-) 105.40
1990-91	2170.90	2190.50	(-) 19.60
1991-92	2447.30	2635.00	(-) 187.70
1992-93	3147.30	3331.30	(-) 164.00
1993-94	3444.40	3626.00	(-) 181.60
TOTAL	25109.38	26066.96	(-) 957.88

Source: (1) Government of Orissa : Statistical Abstract of Orissa, (1969), pp. 395-402. (2) Government of Orissa : Orissa Budget : Some Facts and Charts,(1977-78), pp. 4-29.(3) Government of Orissa : Orissa Budget in brief, (1985-86), pp. 30-33. (4) Government of Orissa : Orissa Budget in Brief, (1993-94), pp. 20-32.

The least square estimate of the above equation for the revenue receipt is :

R_{re} = 40.8935 e0.1302t; R^2= 0.993

Where, R_{re} = Revenue receipts expressed in Rs. crores.

It would be noted from the above equation that the annual compound rate of growth of total revenue receipt during the period is approximately 13.02 percent.

The growth rate of revenue expenditures have also been

carried out by using the same procedure used in case of revenue receipts analysis.

The least square estimate of the said equation ($Y = ae^{rt}$) is :

$$R_{ep} = 44.0845\ e0.1280t;\quad R2= 0.991$$

where, R_{ep} = Revenue expenditure expressed in Rs. crores.

The growth rate of revenue expenditure, during the period is approximately 12.8 percent.

This clearly indicates that the annual compound growth rate of total revenue receipts in the revenue budget is slightly greater than that of revenue expenditures by 0.22 percent and thereby serves to show the relative rigidity of revenue expenditures in the state.

Column 3 of the table indicates the state's over all surplus (+) and deficit (-) in the Revenue Budget for the three decades. It is to be noted that, the budget deficits in recent years has become a permanent feature of state finance. Not only, the state government in recent years has preferred to have a deficit budget but also to have a deficit budget of varying amounts. The huge budget deficits that the state economy experiences may be attributed to a large plan out lay without commensuration of any comprehensive plan programmes to mobilize adequate resources. Further, this poor state of affairs may be attributed to the fact that in an economy, where the per capita income is pathetically low coupled with a large non-monetized sector, the government might be finding it difficult either to expand the tax base or to make an upward revision of its tax rates. In order to find out a suitable answer to the above mentioned vexed problem, it is desirable to have a study of tax responsiveness which has been carried out in the subsequent chapters.

ANALYSIS OF CAPITAL ACCOUNT

The receipts and expenditures of the Orissa state Government on capital account is discussed below. Receipts and expenditures on capital account constitute an important armory of fiscal instruments to affect transfer of resources, though their effect are said to be spilled over a longer period of time. Capital receipts being mainly financed by loans, their impact on the total magnitude of flow of resources is difficult to ascertain. A broad idea of the total magnitude of flow of these resources can be had from the study of the pattern of capital disbursement. It is believed that a well thought out policy of capital receipts and capital expenditure forms the base of economic development in a under developed state like Orissa. The following table 4.2 shows the trends of capital receipts and capital expenditures of the state Government for the years 1961-62 to 1993-94.

Table 4.2 provides the extent to which the growth in capital receipts and capital disbursement of the State Government has taken place in the last thirty-three years. From the above table, it is evident that both the capital receipts and capital expenditures taken separately have increased during the period 1961-62 to 1993-94. The observed trend indicates that there was a marginal surplus in the state budget on capital account amounting to only Rs.12.89 crores. In 1962-63 and 1963-64, there were also marginal deficits of Rs.0.25 crores and Rs.4.25 crores respectively followed by a small surplus of the order of Rs.4.10 crores and Rs.15.88 crores in the two subsequent fiscal years. The budget deficit on capital account during these years was due to infrastructural development in terms of public works and contruction. Again, there was a budget deficit of Rs, 2.42 crores in the year 1966-67. The year 1967-68 began a period of capital surpluses for eight years consequently from 1967-68 to 1974-75. From 1975-76 onwards, there were quite massive deficits in the capital budget up to the year 1982-83. The years 1984-85 and 1986-87 again experienced a budget deficit to the tune of Rs. 32.40 crores and Rs. 95.60 crores respectively. The major factor in the growth of budget deficit in the capital budget of the state during the years 1975-76 to

1982-83 and from 1984-85 to 1986-87 was the expenditures on debt services, which increased tremendously during these years. Further, increasing expenditures under general services , social and economic services was also responsible for the deficit during these years.

TABLE 4.2
CAPITAL BUDGETS OF THE GOVERNMENT OF ORISSA (1961-62 TO 1993-94)

(Rs. in crores)

YEAR	TOTAL CAPITAL RECEIPTS	TOTAL CAPITAL DISBURSEMENT	SURPLUS (+)/ DEFICIT (-)
0	1	2	3
1961-62	124.43	111.54	+ 12.89
1962-63	147.20	147.25	- 0.05
1963-64	178.57	182.82	- 4.25
1964-65	258.74	254.64	+ 4.10
1965-66	256.55	240.67	+ 15.88
1966-67	246.43	248.85	+ 2.42
1967-68	253.49	242.27	+ 11.22
1968-69	307.17	300.04	+ 7.13
1969-70	301.33	291.14	+ 10.19
1970-71	298.51	289.84	+ 8.67
1971-72	362.58	352.49	+ 10.09
1972-73	433.16	423.93	+ 9.23
1973-74	405.93	360.67	+ 45.26
1974-75	391.93	386.42	+ 5.51
1975-76	494.01	506.47	- 12.46
1976-77	588.20	608.20	- 20.00

(Condt..)

0	1	2	3
1977-78	656.40	670.90	- 14.50
1978-79	672.20	724.20	- 52.00
1979-80	803.80	832.10	- 28.30
1980-81	1053.70	1136.60	- 82.90
1981-82	1113.60	1142.40	- 28.80
1982-83	1573.70	1601.00	- 27.30
1983-84	1995.50	1868.30	+127.20
1984-85	1906.70	1939.10	- 32.40
1985-86	2144.60	2007.30	+137.30
1986-87	2184.10	2279.70	- 95.60
1987-88	2647.60	2599.30	+ 48.30
1988-89	2942.40	2791.70	+105.70
1989-90	3061.50	3027.60	+ 33.90
1990-91	3926.10	3776.50	+149.60
1991-92	4429.90	4242.90	+187.00
1992-93	4610.70	4452.70	+158.00
1993-94	4665.20	4483.60	+181.60
TOTAL	45435.93	44515.14	+ 920.79

Source : (1) Government of Orissa : Statistical Abstract of Orissa, (1969), pp. 395-402. (2) Government of Orissa : Orissa Budget : Some Facts and Charts, (1977-78), pp. 4-29 (3) Government of Orissa : Budget in brief, (1985-86), pp. 30-33. (4) Government of Orissa : Orissa Budget in Brief, (1993-94), pp.20-32.

During the entire period covered by the study, capital receipts increased incredibly from Rs. 124.43 crores to Rs. 4665.20 crores registering an average annual rate of increase of 110.58 percent. In contrast, the increase in capital disbursement from Rs. 111.54 crores in 1961-62 to Rs. 4483.60 crores in 1993-94 gives an average annual rate of increase of 118.78 percent. It is evident that the average annual rate of increase in capital expenditures is greater than that of capital receipts. Here, it may be noted that the pattern of growth both in revenue budget as well as in capital budget remain the same.

The tremendous increase in public expenditures on both the account of the state may be ascribed to the following reasons.

The process of public expenditure is the product of a series of 'value judgment' that the society places on it. The quantum of public expenditures is determined by the existing societal needs and aspirations and the political ideology of the party in power. As the public expenditure policies are the logical offshoot of the political ideologies of the various political party/ies in power at a particular period of time. Therefore, these policies of public expenditure are changeable, and some times hard to define. Yet, a general pattern of the policies of public expenditure can be rationalized. These general policies must aim at providing certain services for the social, economic and financial security to the people by way of distributive justice, to promote the most effective utilization of human and other resources by attaining efficient allocation of resources and to maintain a stable terms of trade by achieving economic stability.

The tremendous growth in public expenditure in the state of Orissa can be explined in part due to the implementation of the above objectives. In addition to these forces, multiplication of public wants, the rise of 'welfare estate', the rapid growth of population, the intensities of public expenditure towards economic and social development and the rising prices; might have contributed to the ever increasing growth of public expenditure in the state of Orissa.

The growth rates of capital receipts and capital expenditures have been calculated by following the same formula:

$$Y = ae^{rt}.$$

The least square estimates of the above equations are :

$$C_{re} = 112.1023 \;\; e0.1142t \; ; \; R2 = 0.979$$

$$C_{rp} = 109.8163 \;\; e0.1145 \; ; \; R2 = 0.981$$

where, C_{re} = Capital receipts,

C_{ep} =Capital expenditures

The growth rate in capital receipts is nearly 0.11 (11 percent), while the growth rate in capital expenditures is also approximately 0.11 (11 percent). There does not seem to be any difference between the two growth rates. Thus, the growth in capital revenue is absorbed by the growth in capital expenditures and the former does not add anything substantial to the net surpluses in the capital budget, as they cancel out each other.

OVERALL BUDGETARY POSITION OF THE STATE

Finally, with a view to ascertain an overall or consolidated view of the budgets of the Government of Orissa, during the period under review the surplus/deficit of revenue and capital budgets are shown in Table 4.3.

The overall budgetary trend of the Orissa Government as evident from Table 4.3 clearly indicates a deficit budget in most of the years. The deficit budgets during certain years may be attributed to a poor mobilisation of resources on account of natural calamities coupled with low level of SDP. The state however experienced a surplus budget for certain years (Table 4.3). The surplus budgets during these years are attributed to the better performances of all the sectors and better tax realizations. It is interesting to note that, the surplus or deficit in the Revenue account has more or less, largely been counter-balanced by a deficit or surplus in the capital account or has resulted in a over all deficit or surplus in most of the years.

It would be worthwhile examining the specific features of the state's revenues and expenditures patterns particularly those relating (i) the concomitant movements of state revenues and state incomes; and (ii) the behavior of state's aggregate revenues and expenditures in relation to changes in aggregative economic activity in the state as reflected by estimates of state's Net Domestic Product at factor cost at current prices. The motive to carry out the first exercise is to determine the extent of correlation that exists between state revenues and state incomes. The second part of the enquiry is an attempt to determine the basis for finding out the responsiveness or elasticity of state revenues and expenditures with respect to state income. These two exercices are carried out to lead support to the previous findings with respect to behavior and trends in receipts and expenditures of the state. This would further enable to examine the question, whether the state's revenue/expenditure structure is responsive or not.

TABLE 4.3

SURPLUS/DEFICIT ON REVENUE AND CAPITAL ACCOUNTS OF THE ORISSA STATE GOVERNMENT, 1961-62 TO 1993-94.

(Rs. in crores)

YEAR	EVENUE ACCOUNT SURPLUS(+)/ DEFICIT (-)	CAPITAL ACCOUNT SURPLUS(+) DEFICIT (-)	OVER ALL SURPLUS(+)/ DEFICIT (-)
0	1	2	3
1961-62	- 15.21	+ 12.89	- 2.32
1962-63	- 3.72	- 0.05	- 3.77
1963-64	- 2.72	- 4.25	- 6.97
1964-65	- 4.23	+ 4.10	- 0.13
1965-66	- 10.92	+ 15.88	+ 4.96
1966-67	+ 2.38	- 2.42	- 0.04
1967-68	- 4.17	+ 11.22	+ 7.05
1968-69	- 15.15	+ 7.13	- 8.02
1969-70	+ 0.12	+ 10.19	+ 10.31
1970-71	- 4.06	+ 8.67	+ 4.61
1971-72	- 23.76	+ 10.09	- 13.67
1972-73	- 24.64	+ 9.23	- 15.41
1973-74	- 37.84	+ 45.26	+ 7.42

(Condt..)

0	1	2	3
1974-75	+ 3.86	+ 5.51	+ 9.37
1975-76	+ 1.28	- 12.46	- 11.18
1976-77	+ 17.60	- 20.00	- 2.40
1977-78	+ 27.80	- 14.50	+ 13.30
1978-79	+ 45.10	- 52.00	- 6.90
1979-80	+ 18.70	- 28.30	- 9.60
1980-81	+ 80.80	- 82.90	- 2.10
1981-82	+ 27.90	- 28.80	- 0.90
1982-83	- 23.00	- 27.30	- 50.30
1983-84	+ 0.40	+127.20	+127.60
1984-85	- 73.70	- 32.40	-106.10
1985-86	- 60.10	+137.30	+ 77.20
1986-87	- 19.70	- 95.60	-115.30
1987-88	- 74.50	+ 48.30	- 26.20
1988-89	-107.80	+105.70	- 2.10
1989-90	-105.40	+ 33.90	- 71.50
1990-91	- 19.60	+149.60	+130.00
1991-92	-187.70	+187.00	- 0.70
1992-93	-184.00	+158.00	- 26.00
1993-94	-181.60	+181.60	0.00
TOTAL	- 957.58	+ 920.79	- 36.79

Source: Tables 4.1 and 4.2.

An analysis of coefficient of correlation reveals significant correlations between state's receipts and expenditures, between state's income and state's expenditures on both the current and capital account. The results are summarized in Table 4.4.

TABLE 4.4

COEFFICIENT OF CORRELATION (r)

Variables	On current A/C	On capital A/C
1. Receipts and Expenditures	0.9992	0.9990
2. Receipts and state income	0.9966	0.9816
3. Expenditures and State income	0.9963	0.9804

It is evident that the computed values of *r* in all cases are highly significant and in each case, there is a positive relationship. Further this exhibits that all the conscientiae variable mover in the same direction.

RESPONSIVENESS OF PUBLIC REVENUE AND PUBLIC EXPENDITURE TO STATE INCOME

In this following paragraphs, an attempt is made to examine the behaviour of total state revenues and expenditures in relation to changes in state income (at factor cost) at current prices for finding out the responsiveness (or income elasticity) of public expenditures. For this purpose, we have computed the elasticities of revenues and expenditures on current account with respect to state income for the years 1961-62 to 1993-94, by using the following formula :

$$\Delta X/X_a \div \Delta Y/Y_i = (\Delta X/\Delta Y)/(X_a/Y_i),$$

Where, X_a denotes revenue receipts or expenditures as the case may be and Y_i denotes state income (at factor cost) at current prices in the first period.

In other words, to find out the income elasticity of the revenue receipts and revenue expenditures the following formula has been applied:

$$= \frac{\text{Percentage change in revenue receipts/expenditures}}{\text{percentage change in state income}}$$

It may be noted here that this particular measure has been calculated by relating changes in actual revenue receipts/ expenditures to changes in state income, and to that extent differs from the coefficient of built-in-elasticity, which is calculated with respect only to the automatic increase in revenue receipts/expenditures in response to economic growth or increase in income. Here, the intention is to examine, whether the total relative increase in revenue receipts/ revenue expenditures are due to economic growth or the inherent changes in the structure of revenue receipts and expenditures.

Table 4.5 exhibits the year-wise elasticities of receipts and expenditures on revenue account with respect to state income.

TABLE 4.5

REVENUE AND EXPENDITURE ELASTICITY WITH RESPECT TO STATE INCOME OF ORISSA, 1961-62 TO 1993-94.

(Time-point Elasticity) (Rs. in crores)

YEAR	TOTAL REVENUE RECEIPTS	TOTAL STATE INCOMES	REVENUE ELASTICITY TO STATE INCOME	TOTAL REVENUE EXPENDI TURES	TOTAL STATE INCOME	EXPENDITURE ELASTICITY TO STATE INCOME
0	1	2	3	4	5	6
1961-62	37.20	395.20	0.0000	61.35	395.20	0.0000
1962-63	42.64	490.80	0.6045	65.99	490.80	0.3127
1963-64	46.95	517.40	0.6155	72.01	571.40	0.5555
1964-65	52.35	639.10	0.9708	79.20	639.10	0.8427
1965-66	59.58	625.90	- 6.6868	91.31	625.90	- 7.4031
1966-67	63.58	771.60	0.2884	104.42	771.60	0.6168

(Condt..)

0	1	2	3	4	5	6
1967-68	67.98	868.70	0.5499	113.20	868.70	0.6682
1968-69	77.41	944.30	1.5940	131.77	944.30	1.8850
1969-70	90.20	1023.10	1.9800	131.07	1023.10	- 0.0691
1970-71	96.68	1052.30	2.5948	139.89	1052.30	2.3749
1971-72	07.10	1061.50	12.0662	175.08	1061.50	28.7731
1972-73	119.86	1310.00	0.5089	192.78	1310.00	0.4318
1973-74	130.44	1620.80	0.3721	212.46	1620.80	0.4303
1974-75	145.69	1691.80	2.6689	223.51	1691.80	1.1873
1975-76	188.00	1759.80	7.2253	276.18	1759.80	5.8628
1976-77	204.10	1692.30	- 2.2327	288.30	1692.30	- 1.1441
1977-78	212.40	2110.60	0.1645	319.00	2110.60	0.4308
1978-79	244.60	2216.50	3.0214	378.00	2216.50	3.6861
1979-80	317.70	2250.20	19.6562	448.90	2250.20	12.3365
1980-81	426.10	3095.80	0.9080	540.50	3095.80	0.5430
1981-82	439.30	3568.70	0.2080	573.60	3568.70	0.4009
1982-83	475.30	3599.70	9.4339	824.60	3599.70	50.3748
1983-84	550.50	4818.70	0.4672	782.70	4818.70	- 0.1500
1984-85	632.90	4741.30	- 9.3187	897.20	4741.30	- 9.1075
1985-86	692.20	5652.90	0.4873	1000.90	5652.90	0.6011
1986-87	910.50	5936.70	6.2817	1247.90	5936.70	4.9155
1987-88	945.00	6151.80	1.0458	1407.60	6151.80	3.5321
1988-89	1064.70	7359.60	0.6452	1658.70	7359.60	0.9086
1989-90	1296.00	9104.80	0.9161	1846.10	9104.80	0.4764
1990-91	1564.00	11228.30	0.8866	2190.50	11228.30	0.7999
1991-92	1774.00	12913.20	0.8948	2635.00	12913.20	1.3523
1992-93	2164.20	13446.50	5.3259	3331.30	13446.50	6.3985
1993-94	2405.60	14946.73	0.9998	3626.00	14946.73	0.7929

Source: (For column 1, 2 and column 4) : Government of Orissa, statistical Abstract of Orissa 1969, Orissa Budgets 1977-78, 1985-86, 1993-94. Estimates of State Domestic Product 1950-51 to 1988-89. Economic Survey of Orissa, 1993-94.

Note : Figures presented in column 1 of the above table may not tally with the figures given in Table 4.1, since total revenue receipts shown here does not include grants and contributions from the Union Government.

The negative elasticities on revenue and expenditure accounts revealed by the table for some years may be attributed either to a decline in state incomes during these years as compared to the immediately preceding year or due to some extraneous stimuli. In contrast to this, the high elasticities of revenue receipts and expenditures may be attributed to better tax realization or due to conscious efforts on the part of the government to take away a greater portion of incremental income in to the tax net.

Further, an attempt was made to compare the time point elasticity with the constant point elasticity. An analysis of Constant Base elasticity of revenue receipts and expenditures with respect to state income was carried out with a motive to eliminate the fluctuations in the annual trend value of time point elasticity as it does not eliminate the fluctuations in the current market prices.. The results of our analysis are presented in Table 4.6 below.

The over all result suggests that the values of the elasticity of both the revenue receipts and expenditures are to be less than unity in the initial time period, explaining thereby, the relative inelasticity of the revenue receipts and expenditures to the growth of state income. On the other hand, the elasticities of revenue receipts and expenditures are observed to be more than unity for the later periods thereby exhibiting the relatively elastic nature of both revenue receipts and expenditures to the state income. So, the question arises; why this is so?

We apprehend, that we may not be able to offer any suitable economic explanation to the question posed above.

The most Plausible explanation for the low income elasticities of revenue receipts (for the years 1962-63 to 1974-75) as evident from our analysis, might be due to low level of economic activities in the state, that have a bearing on the taxable capacity of the economy on the one hand and relative tax efforts of the state Government on the other hand.

TABLE 4.6

REVENUE AND EXPENDITURE ELASTICITY WITH RESPECT TO STATE INCOME OF ORISSA, 1961-62 TO 1993-94.

(CONSTANT-BASE ELASTICITY)

YEAR	REVENUE ELASTICITY TO STATE INCOME	EXPENDITURE ELASTICITY TO STATE INCOME
0	1	2
1961-62	0.0000	0.0000
1962-63	0.6045	0.3127
1963-64	0.5879	0.3897
1964-65	0.6599	0.4714
1965-66	1.0306	0.8366
1966-67	0.7446	0.7371
1967-68	0.6906	0.7054
1968-69	0.7780	0.8261
1969-70	0.8967	0.7147
1970-71	0.9649	0.7699
1971-72	1.1145	1.0995
1972-73	0.9599	0.9255
1973-74	0.8082	0.7942
1974-75	0.8889	0.8056
1975-76	1.1740	1.0141
1976-77	1.3670	1.1271
1977-78	1.0850	0.9675
1978-79	1.2098	1.1200
1979-80	1.6064	1.3458
1980-81	1.5299	1.1429

(Condt...)

0	1	2
1981-82	1.3461	1.0398
1982-83	1.4524	1.5343
1983-84	1.2328	1.0505
1984-85	1.4561	1.2389
1985-86	1.3235	1.1511
1986-87	1.6742	1.3793
1987-88	1.6753	1.5065
1988-89	1.5674	1.4775
1989-90	1.5354	1.3200
1990-91	1.4973	1.2661
1991-92	1.4740	1.3244
1992-93	1.7314	1.6139
1993-94	1.7291	1.5780

Note: Calculations are based on Table 4.5.

Based on the similar logic, we may argue, that the state's inability to mobilise adequate resources, subjected to the constraint of low level of taxable capacity might have restrained the state Government from undertaking further developmental plan programmes during these years (i.e. from 1962-63 to 1974-75), which might have been one of the factors for the inelasticity character of public expenditures in the state.

On the other hand, the state experienced a elastic trend of revenue receipts and expenditure, from 1975-76 to 1993-94. These trends conform to the general theoretical argument that with the gradual commercialization, and modernization of the state economy, it has been possible for the state Government to increase the taxable capacity as well as its level of public expenditure. Further, we may note that the price revolution brought about by the market forces has also significantly altered the relative importance of both revenue and expenditure in the fiscal structure of the state thereby explains the above trend to a reasonable extent.

The constant Base elasticity of revenue receipts and expenditures in the analysis gives some important findings. It is observed from the foregoing Table 4.6, that, the elastiity values of the revenue receipts were relatively greater than the corresponding elasticity values of expenditures. These data lend some support to the general impression that with the growth and commercialization of the economy, the State Government found itself in a better position to exploit the internal sources of revenue to finance its various developmental expenditures during the years 1975-76 to 1993-94.

It would be worth explaining the nature of the curve of the time-point elasticity and constant-base elasticity of revenue receipts and expenditures that broadly emerges from our analysis.

We have represented graphically the values of time-point elasticity and constant-base elasticity for the purpose of comparison and to know the actual magnitude of the trend of the values of elasticity. The X-axis represents the year and the Y-axis represents the values of elasticity of revenue receipts/expenditures (as the case may be).

Graph-I, exhibits the trend of elasticities of revenue receipts and, Graph-II, shows the trend of elasticities of revenue expenditures.

All these two graphs of revenue receipts and expenditures exhibit more or less the same pattern and amplitude. We can only infer that changes in revenue receipts and expenditures are very sensitive to changes in state income. As, we have seen here from the monotonic nature of the two graphs, we can conclude that both receipts and expenditures are more influenced by income rather than by changing bases in case of receipts and by some other factors in case of expenditures. We may also add that this could happen only when there is a very steady growth rate in the state income without any catrastrophy or disaster.

No attempt has been made to analyse the contributory factors to the consistency of ups and downs in both the curves since they largely fall outside the purview of this chapter. Their analysis needs further research and an indepth study into the problem.

It is thought imperative to undertake an analysis of the elasticity of aggregate public expenditure of both revenue and capital account with respect to state income.

There are two points, which are note worthy about the forgoing analysis.

Firstly, when the time-point elasticity of total public expenditure with respect to state income was calculated, it was found that the values of the elasticity for public expenditures are of the same pattern with almost the same amplitude unlike that of revenue expenditures. Correspondingly, the values of the elasticity of total expenditure are reported to be relatively greater than those of the values of the elasticity of revenue expenditures. This substantiates the earlier findings that the capital expenditures are more flexible to state income in comparison to revenue expenditures.

Secondly, the result of the constant-base elasticity of the foregoing Table 4.6 indicates that public expenditures are highly responsive to changes in state income. This is evident from the values of the public expenditure elasticity, where it stayed more than unity for almost the entire period covered by our study with the exception to the two initial time periods, i.e. from 1962-63 to 1963-64, and in 1970-71 and 1973-74 to 1974-75 where the values of elasticity are observed to be less than unity. On an average, total expenditures have been growing faster than the state income as evident from the table. This clearly exhibits that there has been a shift in state's composition of public expenditure towards capital expenditures.

Figure I Trend of Elasticities of Revenue Receipts

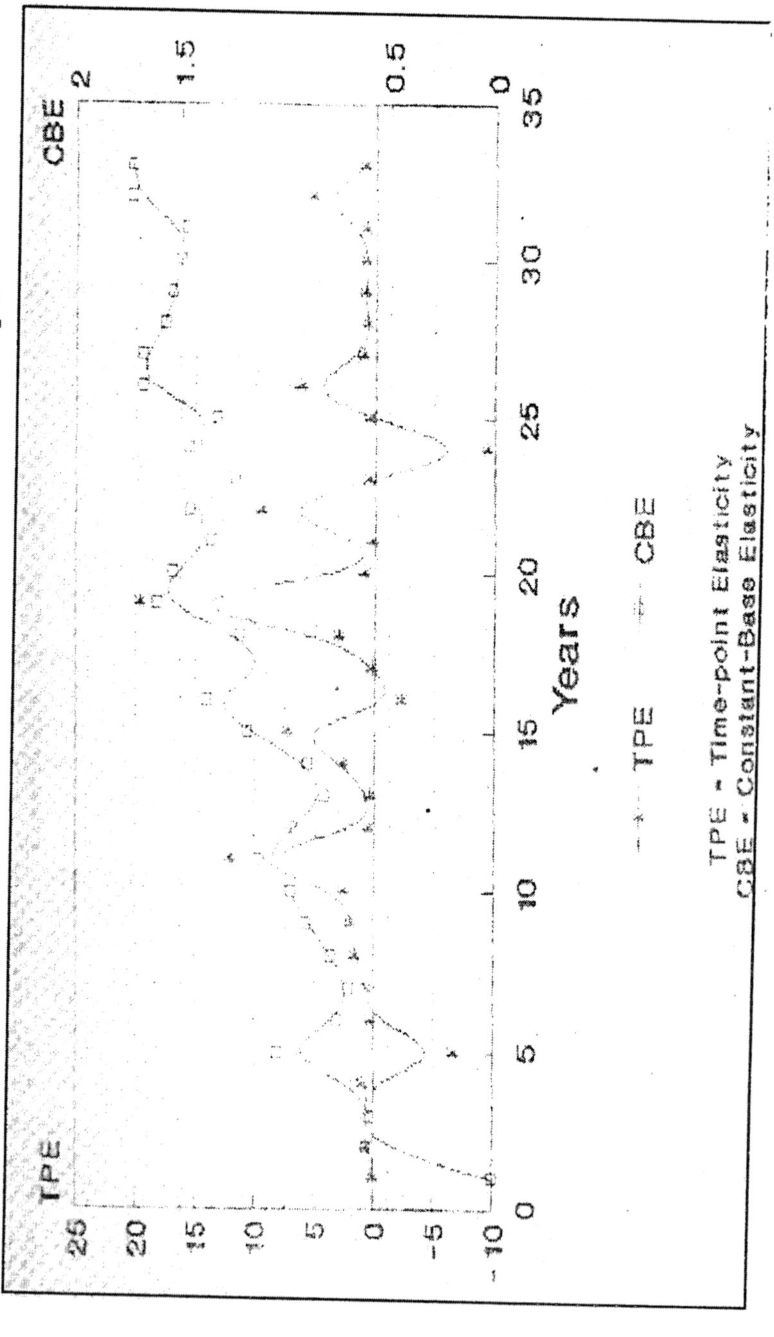

Figure II Trend of Elasticities of Revenue Expenditures

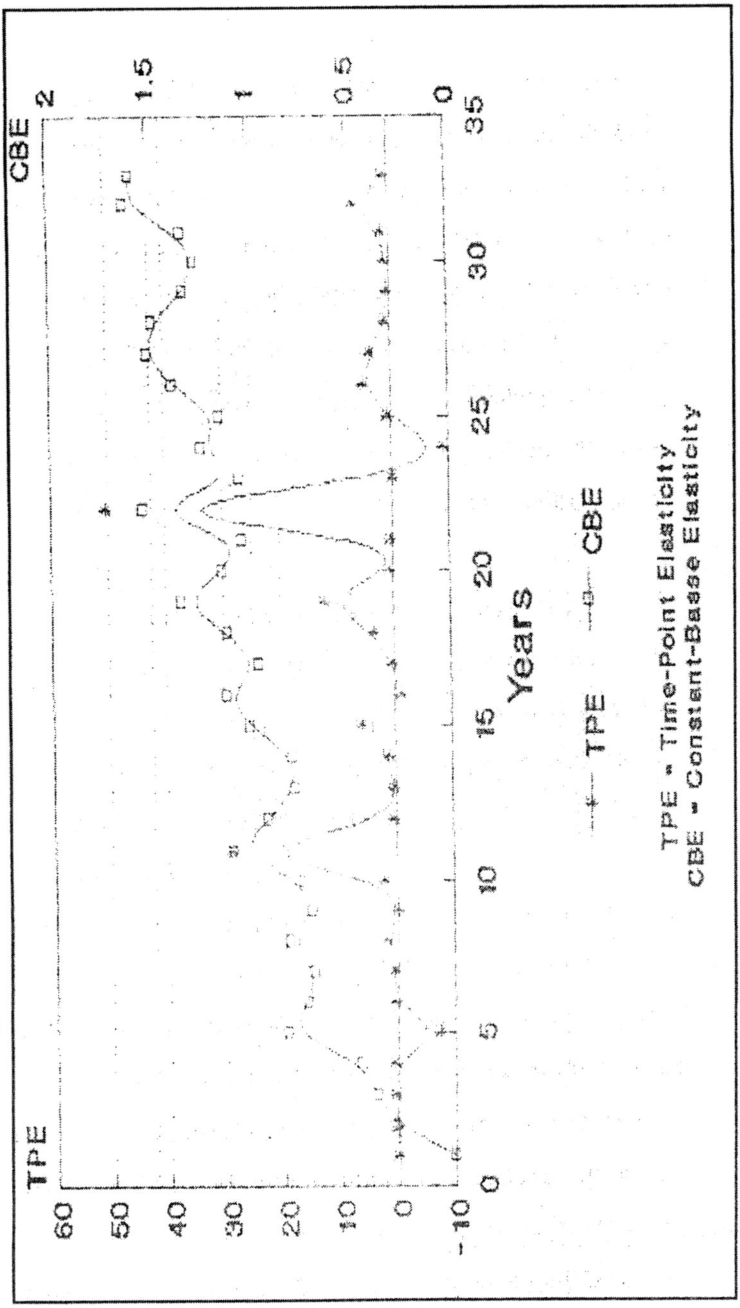

TABLE 4.7

TOTAL PUBLIC EXPENDITURES (BOTH REVENUE AND CAPITAL ACCOUNT) ELASTICITY WITH RESPECT TO STATE INCOME OF ORISSA, 1961-62 TO 1993-94

(Rs. in crores)

YEAR	TOTAL EXPEND ITURES	TOTAL STATE INCOME	EXPENDITURE ELASTICITY TO STATE INCOME *	EXPENDITURE ELASTICITY TO STATE INCOME **
0	1	2	3	4
1961-62	82.97	395.20	0.000	0.000
1962-63	100.46	490.80	0.871	0.871
1963-64	115.19	571.40	0.893	0.871
1964-65	144.41	639.16	2.141	1.201
1965-66	166.49	625.90	- 7.403	1.724
1966-67	177.53	771.60	0.285	1.197
1967-68	200.53	868.70	1.030	1.183
1968-69	274.55	944.30	4.241	1.662
1969-70	237.67	1023.10	- 1.610	1.173
1970-71	206.84	1052.30	- 4.545	0.898
1971-72	265.53	1061.50	32.455	1.305
1972-73	337.45	1310.00	1.157	1.325
1973-74	313.50	1620.80	- 0.299	0.896
1974-75	306.24	1691.80	- 0.529	0.82
1975-76	452.19	1759.80	11.857	1.289

(Condt..)

0	1	2	3	4
1976-77	581.50	1692.30	- 7.455	1.831
1977-78	675.20	2110.60	0.652	1.645
1978-79	622.90	2216.50	- 1.544	1.412
1979-80	620.40	2250.20	- 0.264	1.380
1980-81	889.30	3095.80	1.153	1.422
1981-82	1058.00	3568.70	1.242	1.463
1982-83	1409.50	3599.70	38.246	1.972
1983-84	1915.30	4818.70	1.060	1.973
1984-85	1844.60	4741.30	2.298	1.931
1985-86	1716.30	5652.90	- 0.362	1.481
1986-87	1954.80	5936.70	2.768	1.609
1987-88	2511.10	6151.80	7.854	2.009
1988-89	2899.30	7359.60	0.787	1.926
1989-90	3006.00	9104.80	0.155	1.599
1990-91	3679.20	11228.30	0.960	1.581
1991-92	4272.10	12913.20	1.074	1.594
1992-93	5459.40	13446.50	6.729	1.962
1993-94	5529.80	14946.73	0.116	1.783

NOTE : *Calculations based on Time-point Elasticity. **Calculations based on constant-based Elasticity.

Source: (for column 1 and 2) : Government of Orissa, Statistical Abstract of Orissa : 1969, Orissa Budgets in Brief : 1977-78, 1985-86, 1993-94, Estimate of State Domestic Product 1950-51 to 1988-89, Economic survey of Orissa, 1993-94.

Thus, the results obtained suggest that during the particular period covered by the study, deliberate effort on the part of the state Governments accounted for a substantial part of the variations in the value of the coefficient for the total public expenditures.

The graphical representation of time-point elasticity and constant-base elasticity of public expenditures is shown in Graph 3.

What we could gather from time-point elasticity, that there is almost a monotonous trend. Sometimes, we may wonder whether the effect of trend is anywhere relevant except in two occasions, i.e. in the years 1971-72 and 1982-83. So, there is a monotonous trend for a period of ten years from 1961-62 onwards, upto 1970-71. Then it took an exceptional jump in the year 1971-72 and thereafter again it became stable and until ten years i.e. upto 1981-82; after that, again there is a jump in the year 1982-83. And, since then, until the year 1994, the trend is peculiarly stable. Therefore, these particular two years which has a positive higher trend must have to be accounted by some other factors. But, this kind of trend which is almost parallel to base does not give so much high expectation about the growth or decline in public expenditures.

Regarding constant-base elasticity which is calculated by using traditional method, but we have circumvented by taking the base year's 1961-62 value of public expenditure as the base year to calculate the constant base elasticity. Naturally, index numbers always increase even if, public expenditure is not increasing in a remarkable way. As a result, we expect to have the elasticity of the succeeding years to rise high and high to give us the notion of the trend and this is exactly what has been observed in Graph 3. But, one advantage of the so called constant-base elasticity (CBE)

Figure III
Trend of Elasticities of Publuc Expenditures (Revenue and Capital)

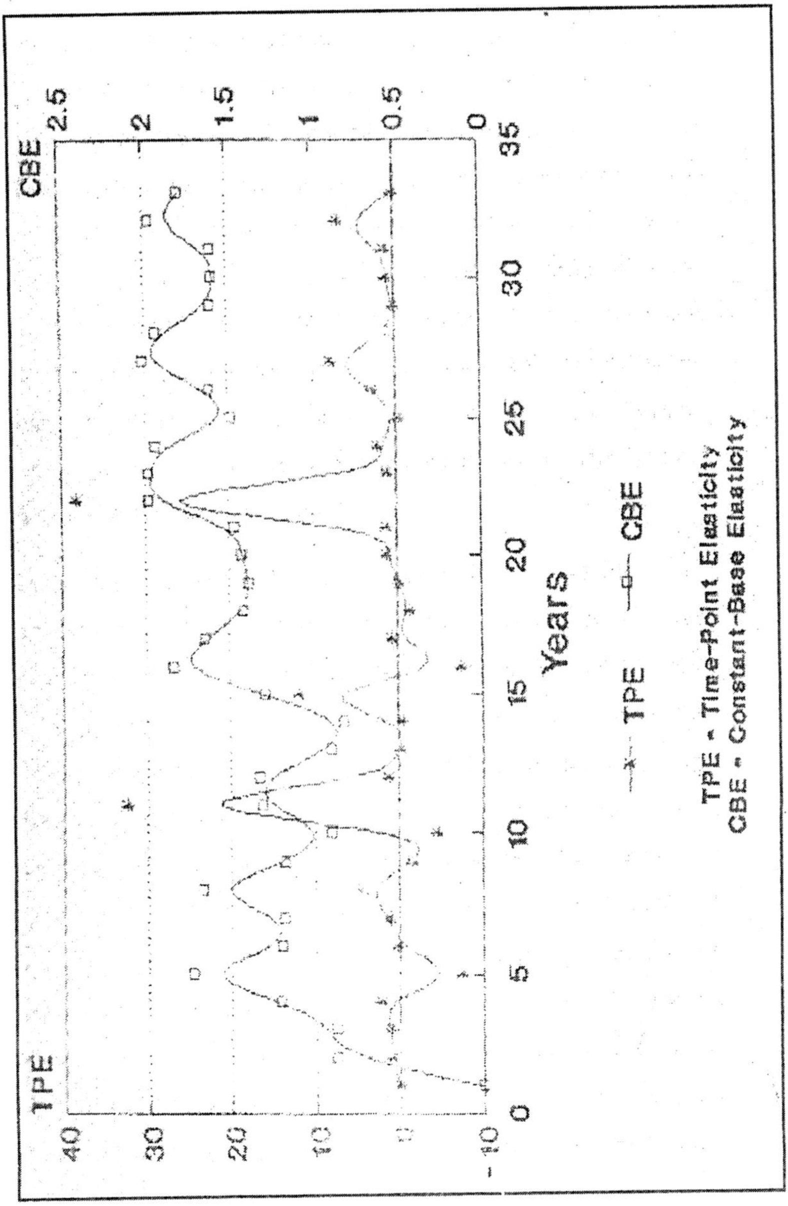

in our opinion is that, inspite of the fact of using the indices, it should have been all the times in the rising pattern rather than declining sometimes or again increasing sometimes. This phenomena partly, may be attributed to the spill over effect.

Incidentally, it is observed that, the consistency in ups and downs in both the curves represented in Graph 3, are similar to those of the curves represented in Graph 2. At this juncture of our analysis, we thought it imperative to provide some explanations towards the cause of these trends.

It is an established fact that, whenever we are having a series of data, the trend is looked after by the empirical regression equation itself. In this case, we may mention the constant term of the regression equation, which is nothing but a contributor to the consistency of ups and downs in either public expenditures or income. Further, we believe that the consistency of ups and downs in both these curves might be due to the existence of a strong and positive correlation between the public expenditure and state income. To substantiate it, we carried out a simple linear regression equation of the type.

The regression of total public expenditures (Pe) on the state income (Y) yields the following value :

$$Pe = -133.6018 + 0.3736\ Y$$

$$R2 = 0.9832$$

It was found that public expenditures, both revenue and capital, explain near abut 98.32 percent of the state income of Orissa. The computed value of coefficient of correlation (r) was worked out to be 0.9915, which clearly shows a very significant correlation between public expenditures and state income. Hence, our arguments in the foregoing paragraph are largely substantiated by our empirical data.

We have suspected however that due to the inherent nature of time-series data, it is possible that the disturbance vector might be autocorrelated. To test this, we have estimated the Durbinwatson statistic. The value of DW is 1.71. This shows that our suspicion has no ground for support. Hence, our analysis in estimating the above equation is not vitiated by auto-correlated disturbances.

4.6. CONCLUDING REMARKS

One of the most distressing features of the state finance, that emerges from our study is the growing volume of revenue deficits in recent years. The continuous outpacing of the growth of revenues both in the eighties and nineties has led to serious deterioration in the state's budgetary positions, from a surplus of 1.32 percent of Net State Domestic Product in the mid-seventies (i.e. in 1977-78) to a deficit of about 1.22 percent of Net State Domestic Product in 1993-94. In absolute terms, the net revenue deficits in 1993-94 was close to Rs. 181.60 crores.

Since 1982-83, dissaving has been showing large increases year after year mainly due to very high growth of revenue expenditures. The increase in expenditures has been particularly alarming in 1984-85 when it grew at an average rate of 14.63 percent per annum. What is more with the interest liability itself growing at 23.29 percent per year, expenditure growth has become self-propelling. Equally causing grave concern is the high growth of wages and salaries and subsidies.

Thus, the higher growth of revenue expenditure in relation to the growth of revenue receipts has created an explosive cycle of expenditure growth. The use of borrowed funds for meeting revenue expenditure while increasing interest liability does not create corresponding sources of revenue. In addition, even the borrowed funds used for capital spending are not efficiently utilised. Consequently, interest liabilities feed back into the growth of diversion of borrowed funds. Due to this, the state's gross interest payments during the decade of 1990's grew at the average annual rate of 47.23 percent. Clearly, such a high growth rate of interest payment expenditure is unsustainable.

If, we assume that the observed trend in revenue expenditure will continue into the future in the medium term, then, in order to phase out the revenue deficits in the next four years, i.e. by 1998-1999, the revenue growth would have to accelerate by almost 3.36 percentage points to 10.02 percent per annum. This is indeed a unjustified estimation and therefore immediate remedial measures either to increase the tax effort or to compress the expenditures must be undertaken. The latter proposition may not be a reasonable strategy in case of an most underdeveloped economy like Orissa, where Government assumes the role of a public sector in order to accelerate the tempo of economic development through its various developmental and non-developmental plan expenditure programme. Thus, the massive participation of the Government in developmental and welfare activities has given rise to the problem of Resource constraint. Resource constraints can be judged interms of predominant agricultural sector, low monetization, low industrialization, structural and industrial rigidities, low taxable capacity of the people and so on. But, these constraints are continually minimized as the process of development gets momentum through the structural and institutional changes in the economy. So, the question arises, to what extent, Orissa's tax structure responds to these changes which are inevitable in the process of economic development ? This calls for a more detailed analysis of composition and structure of current revenues of the state Government. This is undertaken in the next chapter.

NOTES AND REFERENCES

1. Government of Orissa; An Economic-cum-purpose classification of the Orissa Government Budget, 1980-81 to 1989-90, Bhubeneswar, Directorate of Economics and Statistics, (1992), pp. 1-20.
2. *Ibid.*, pp. 65-66.

CHAPTER - V

PROBLEM OF RESOURCE CONSTRAINT AND PROSPECTS OF INTERNAL RESOURCE MOBILIZATION

INTRODUCTION

The previous chapter was an attempt to analyse the tax-expenditure policies in terms of the trends and patterns of the Orissa's total revenue receipts and expenditures, for a period of more than three decades covered by our study. And, we found that higher growth of expenditures in relation to the growth of revenue receipts has created an explosive cycle of expenditure growth. This has necessiated the state Government to increase its tax revenues to a considerable extent. The willingness and capacity of the Government to respond to this need has been an important determinant to its capacity to carry forward development plan programmes. In working out a development plan, a major question that nearly always arises is how much tax revenue the state can reasonably expect to raise and from what sources, this should come. No doubt, this calls forth the institutionalization of tax reform. In other words, tax policy has to be made a part of the instrument of developmental goals. It may be noted that the size of Government's development programme is largely determined by the tax yielding capacity of the tax system to mobilize the necessary economic surplus. This policy has to be equally supplemented by such measures which help to keep the recurring and non-productive expenditures at the minimum level thereby making the mobilization of economic surplus, a smooth process.

In an underdeveloped economy like Orissa, economic progress requires in the initial stages that higher proportion of this surplus be channeled into productive investment through various measures of taxation. As such, tax structure should be so designed as to prevent consumption from increasing proportionately with income in the earlier stages of development. To accomplish this objective, a major question that arises; What should be the economic capacity of taxation? Of course, it is not possible to give a definite answer to this question. As M. Douglas (1953) argues[1], "The elements of taxable capacity prove on closer examination to be so contingent, subjective and variable - to be so much a matter of circumstances of time and place, of institutional arrangements, and public attitudes-that they defy generalization, and any conclusion expressed in absolute or final terms is bound to misrepresent the very nature of the problem itself". On the other hand, according to F. Due (1973)[2], "The actual effects of taxation as source of revenue depend upon the type of tax structure the relationship of marginal to average tax rates, the reaction of the tax payers to the high rate, and the length of the period the high rates are effective, etc."

However, in the absence of any rational long-term policy objectives accompanied by non-significant structural changes in Orissan economy, the resource problem has been a measure policy issue.

THRUST OF THE PROBLEM

Therefore, an attempt is made in this chapter to examine the problem of resource constraint and prospects of internal resource mobilization in the state during the last thirty-three years of planning covered by the study. We would explain the revenue constraints and the problem of resource mobilization in terms of existing contribution of different taxes (current revenue) by reflecting their share in the Net State Domestic Product and compositional and structural character of different taxes (current revenue) on the basis of ratios and trends as well.

It may be noted that the tax effort of any state in India depends upon two sets of interdependent factors : First, how effectively the state in question exploits the taxing power assigned to it through its various tax mobilization programmes. No doubt, the existing market structure plays a decisive role in the tax mobilization efforts of the state. Second, the quantum and types of federal transfer it receives. These factors are interdependent and self defeating in the sense that excessively large federal transfers to a state may dampen its effort to attain financial self-reliance thus giving rise to a dependency syndrome on the part of the state. The resultant out come may be: for economically weaker states, tax effort is likely to fall below what relative taxable capacity which would otherwise have made it possible for the state to attain. How these interdependent factors can make an integrated approach in the Orissan context is the focus of this chapter.

It is believed that information on this relationship will be quite useful in making a assessment of the relative tax efforts on the part of the Government. It will also enable us to draw conclusions regarding the specific directions in which the compositional pattern of taxation has moved. This chapter is divided into two parts:

The first part discusses the various aspects of different taxes of the state Government in details, including its resource mobilization capacity in the near future. A brief assessment of shared taxes and other financial resources and there relative importance has also been made. In part II of the chapter, we attempt to examine the size and composition of all types of federal transfers to the state in order to determine their magnitude in the overall fiscal armory of the state. We attempt such an evaluation, in a summary manner.

PART - I

PROBLEM OF INTERNAL RESOURCE MOBILIZATION

In this section, an attempt is made to examine the trends in the revenue yields from different taxes and also their relative place in the system of taxation. An analysis of the overall composition of tax revenue including the shared taxes of the state Government from the beginning of 1961-62 to 1993-94, has also been made.

It is intended to study the composition of tax revenues or the relative importance of the specified individual taxes in the tax system in terms of, either the percentage of different taxes in total tax revenue or the ratio of these taxes to Net State Domestic Product.

The first alternative brings out clearly the differences in the patterns of taxation in the state irrespective of the level of total taxation, whereas the second throws light on the proportion of Gross State Domestic Product collected through different tax forms. These two aspects of changes are of course inter-related. A significant change in tax ratio for instance, almost invariably involves, or, is accompanied by a shift in the composition of taxes.

An attempt is made to discuss the changes in the level and composition of taxation separately, with a view to identify the elements that are to be considered in any analysis of their inter-relationship. While it does not necessarily imply that the proper policy for the state Government is to increase the share of income channeled into public sector, it is believed that, an enquiry of this nature besides throwing some light on the underlining forces at work would be found useful in evaluating actual and potential performances of the state Government in the matter of resource mobilization.

FEASIBLE TRENDS IN TAX EFFORT

Before going into the details of the individual tax items of the State and of the Union (shared taxes), an examination of their combined yields vis-à-vis state income in current prices is essential, because these give an overall idea about the extent to which the state Government has been able to divert additional income into the Public Sector savings. This, no doubt, will exhibit the relative tax effort of the Government. Table 5.1 and 5.2 facilitate such an analysis.

The compound growth rates were worked out using the exponential function of the type :

$$Y = ae^{rt},$$

where, t = time, Y = the dependent variable and
r = growth rate.

Table 5.1 presents year-wise figures of tax revenues and state income at current prices during 1961-62 to 1993-94

Column 2 of the table indicates the state's own tax revenue since 1961-62. This shows that during the span of the past thirty-three years plan period; states own tax revenue has increased in absolute terms, roughly eighty eight-fold, from Rs. 10.35 crores in 1961-62 to Rs. 916.10 crores in 1993-94. Judged by the familiar exponential growth rate, state's own tax revenue has registered a growth rate of 13.86 percent per annum over the years. This increase of state's own tax revenue over the years was mainly due to large receipts under taxes on vehicles, taxes on electricity, state's excise duty and sales tax, all of which have increased considerably over these years. The increase in absolute terms of these taxes may be attributed to the extension of tax base and tax coverage of these taxes and also due to an upward revision of the tax rates during these years.

Column 3 of the table shows the trend of total tax revenue of the state for more than three decades starting from the year 1961-62. Tax revenues shows a rising trend through out the period from 1961-62 to 1993-94, increasing from Rs. 16.87 crores in 1961-62 to Rs. 1953.70 crores in 1993-94, that is, an increase of about one hundred and sixteen-fold during these years. This increase can mainly be attributed to increasing economic activities over a period of time in terms of enhanced level of consumption, production and exchange.

It would also be noted that the annual compound rate of growth of total tax revenue during the period is approximately 14.69 percent.

In column 4, is presented the state income the Net State Domestic Product (NSDP). The data presented is the aggregate of the sector wise estimates by industrial origin of the State Domestic Product at factor cost at current prices.

During the decade, the SDP had increased in absolute terms, roughly thirty-eight fold, from Rs. 395.20 crores in 1961-62 to Rs. 14946.73 crores in 1993-94. The annual compound rate of growth during these periods is about 10.89 percent. This increase in state income during these years may be attributed to the relative greater contribution of the secondary and tertiary sector to the state income.

If, the relationship between the tax revenues and state income is expressed in the conventional tax-income ratio terms, Table 4.1 reveals some interesting results.

In column 6, is shown the percentage of total tax revenue to the state income. This reveals that there existed a continuous rise over the time period. From mere 4.27 percent during 1961-62, it has increase the level of 12.59 percent in the year 1993-94. Thus, this column substantiates the inference that during the last thirty-three years more than proportionate share in incremental state income has been transferred to the hands of the public exchequer.

Column 5, of the table shows an encouraging fact, substantiating what has been pointed out in the previous paragraph. In this column, the percentage of state's own tax revenue to the State's Domestic Product over the years is presented. The percentage of state's own tax revenue to state's income which was 2.62 percent in 1961-62 has increased over the years and was near about 6.13 percent in the year 1993-94. The state's own tax revenue has been moving in the same direction as the increase in the state's income. State's own tax revenue as a percentage of total tax of the state shows a declining trnd. The raio which was 0.61 in the year 1961-62 has decreased over the years to 0.47 in the year 1993-94. The decreasing ratio between own tax revenue to state's total tax revenue spells out that the state has not put in greater efforts than before in raising its own tax revenue in much more efficient way during the last three decades and has not tapped more resources from the state economy thereby not increasing the avenues for financing its own expenditures.

From the table given below, we may draw the following inferences:

(i) First, the increasing state income has been out-paced by both the increasing state's own tax revenue and total tax revenue over the period.

(ii) Second, the role of the state's own tax revenue as an element of state income over the period (1961-62 to 1993-94) has not been commensurate with the expected drive for additional taxation as a source of revenue for the state. Because the percentage share of state's own tax revenue in state income has increased at a much slower pace than the pace assigned to total tax revenue.

(iii) Third, if, tax-income ratio can be taken as a simplest measure of tax burden or sacrifice, then the analysis reveals that the state's tax burden has increased to a very great extent and any increase in further taxation would be counter productive. If the relative tax burden can be taken as an indicator of the relative tax effort of the state, then Orissa emerges rather poorly, and

(iv) Lastly, the analysis also indicates that the state has been relying more and more on shared taxes for the purpose of resource mobilization in comparison to its own sources of revenue. This is nothing but the dependency syndrome that the state experiences in recent years. For a healthy fiscal scenario, this particular trend needs to be reversed.

This entire trend noted above, is substantiated by the observations that we may feel tempted to make on the basis of our study of Table 5.2.

It is observed from the foregoing Table 5.2 that the rate of growth of state's own tax revenue is much lower than the rate of growth of the state's share in central taxes. Yet, the increasing importance of tax revenue as an element of state income has been clearly discernible over the period in question.

Column 7 of the table shows the ratio of the state's own tax revenue to the total tax revenues accruing to the state during these years. A distressing feature regarding this is that, the ratio which was 0.61 in the year 1961-62, decreased to 0.47 in the year 1993-94. The share of shared taxes in the total revenue of the state increased from 17.53 percent in the year 1961-62 to 47.29 percent in the year 1993-94. Unfortunately enough, the dependence of the state on the non-tax revenue as a source of revenue has been more than offset by the revenue from shared taxes, even though it is an interval source of revenue by itself.

By looking at the columns 6 and 8 of the Table 5.2, one can find that the relative importance of state's own taxes has been much less than it has been in the case of shared taxes as an element of total revenue of the state over the period in question.

Further, it is interesting to note that the relative importance of state's own tax revenue has demonstrated a somewhat erratic behaviour though; it has registered a trend towards an increase, from 27.82 percent in the year 1961-62 to 36.36 percent in 1992-93. This clearly shows the increasing dependence of the state on the central devolutions that the state consciously carries out when compared to its otherwise increasing stress on its own tax revenue.

Thus, judged by its own effort, in the last three decades, Orissa's revenue performance has been rather dismal in the sense that the state raised a lower proportion of revenue in comparison to other sources of revenue, viz.; shared taxes.

TABLE 5.1
TAX REVENUE AND STATE INCOME OF ORISSA

(Rs. in crores)

Year	State's Own Tax Revenue	Total Tax Revenue	State Income*	Column 2 as Percentage of Column 4	Column 3 as Percentage of Column 4	Column 2 as a ratio of Column 3
1	2	3	4	5	6	7
1961-62	10.35	16.87	395.20	2.62	4.27	0.61
1962-63	13.34	23.70	490.80	2.72	4.83	0.56
1963-64	16.38	28.52	571.40	2.87	4.99	0.57
1964-65	18.80	30.60	639.10	2.94	4.79	0.61
1965-66	19.62	32.62	625.90	3.13	5.21	0.60
III-Plan Average	15.69	26.46	544.48	2.88	4.81	0.59
1966-67	21.18	36.25	771.60	2.74	4.70	0.58
1967-68	24.21	40.73	868.70	2.79	4.69	0.59

(Condt..)

1	2	3	4	5	6	7
1968-69	26.06	46.05	944.30	2.76	4.88	0.57
Annual Plan Average	23.82	41.01	861.53	2.76	4.76	0.58
1969-70	28.40	53.65	1023.10	2.78	5.24	0.53
1970-71	33.25	63.71	1052.30	3.16	6.05	0.52
1971-72	34.79	72.36	1061.50	3.28	6.82	0.48
1972-73	39.95	82.02	1310.00	3.05	6.26	0.49
1973-74	42.21	88.62	1620.80	2.60	5.47	0.48
IV-Plan Average	35.72	72.07	1213.54	2.94	5.94	0.49
1974-75	50.41	97.66	1691.80	2.98	5.77	0.52
1975-76	68.42	129.88	1759.80	3.89	7.38	0.53
1976-77	80.80	146.00	1692.30	4.77	8.63	0.55
1977-78	83.70	153.10	2110.60	3.97	7.25	0.55
V-Plan Average	70.83	131.66	1813.63	3.90	7.26	0.54
1978-79	98.40	174.10	2216.50	4.44	7.85	0.57
1979-80	112.10	256.40	2250.20	4.98	11.39	0.44
Annual Plan Average	105.25	215.25	2233.35	4.71	9.64	0.49
1980-81	132.60	292.60	3095.80	4.28	9.45	0.45
1981-82	165.60	346.30	2568.70	4.64	9.70	0.48
1983-84	207.20	429.90	4818.70	4.30	8.92	0.48
1984-85	234.90	519.00	4741.30	4.95	10.95	0.45
VI-Plan Average	183.80	392.74	3964.84	4.64	9.91	0.47
1985-86	285.90	561.40	5652.90	5.06	9.93	0.51
1986-87	337.80	752.20	5936.70	5.69	12.67	0.45
1987-88	386.70	788.90	6151.80	6.29	12.82	0.49
1988-89	442.70	871.40	7359.60	6.02	11.84	0.51
1989-90	524.80	1097.40	9104.80	5.76	12.05	0.48

(Condt..)

1	2	3	4	5	6	7
VII-Plan Average	395.58	814.26	6841.16	5.78	11.90	0.49
1990-91	668.80	1362.90	11228.30	5.96	12.14	0.49
1991-92	673.70	1504.20	12913.20	5.22	11.65	0.45
1992-93	787.00	1795.80	13446.50	5.85	13.36	0.44
1993-94	916.10	1953.70	14946.73	6.13	13.07	0.47
VIII-Plan Average upto 4th year	761.40	1654.15	13133.68	5.80	12.59	0.46

Source: Government of Orissa, Statistical Abstract of Orissa (for various years), Orissa Budget in Brief (for various years)

Note: *State Income Figures are in current prices.

GROWTH RATE : Column 2 = 8.786 + 0.13867t, R2= 0.993, Column 3 = 14.9067 + 0.14699t, R2= 0.995

Column 4 = 365.8613 + 0.1089t, R2= 0.989.

TABLE 5.2
PERCENTAGE SHARE OF STATE'S OWN TAX REVENUE, SHARE TAXES AND NON-TAX REVENUE OF ORISSA

Year	State's Own Tax Revenue	Non-Tax Revenue	Shared Taxes	Total Revenue	Column 2 as a % of Column 5	Column 3 as a % of Column 5	Column 4 as a % of Column 3
1	2	3	4	5	6	7	8
1961-62	10.35	20.33	6.52	37.20	27.82	54.65	17.53
1962-63	13.34	18.94	10.36	42.64	31.29	44.42	24.30
1963-64	16.38	18.43	12.14	46.95	34.89	39.25	25.86
1964-65	18.80	21.75	11.80	52.35	35.91	41.55	22.54
1965-66	19.62	26.96	13.00	59.58	32.93	45.25	21.82
IIIrd. Plan Average	15.69	21.28	10.76	47.73	32.87	44.58	22.55
1966-67	21.18	27.33	15.07	63.58	33.31	42.99	23.70
1967-68	24.21	27.25	16.52	67.98	35.61	40.09	24.30
1968-69	26.06	31.36	19.99	77.41	33.66	40.51	25.82

(Condt..)

1	2	3	4	5	6	7	8
Annual Plan							
Average	23.82	28.65	17.19	69.66	34.19	41.13	24.68
1969-70	28.40	36.55	25.25	90.20	31.49	40.52	27.99
1970-71	33.25	33.17	30.46	96.88	34.32	34.24	31.44
1971-72	34.79	34.74	37.57	107.10	32.48	32.44	35.08
1972-73	39.95	37.84	42.07	119.86	33.33	31.57	35.10
1973-74	42.21	41.82	46.41	130.44	32.36	32.06	35.58
IV Plan							
Average	35.72	36.82	36.35	108.89	32.80	33.81	33.38
1974-75	50.41	48.03	47.25	145.69	34.60	32.97	32.43
1975-76	68.42	58.12	61.46	188.00	36.39	30.91	32.69
1976-77	80.80	58.10	65.20	204.10	39.59	28.47	31.95
1977-78	83.70	59.30	69.40	212.40	39.41	27.92	32.67
V Plan							
Average	70.83	55.89	60.83	187.55	37.77	29.80	32.43
1978-79	98.40	70.50	75.70	244.60	40.23	28.83	30.95
1979-80	112.10	61.30	144.30	317.70	35.28	19.29	45.42
Annual Plan							
Average	105.25	65.90	110.00	281.15	37.44	23.44	39.12
1980-81	132.60	133.50	160.00	426.10	31.12	31.33	37.55
1981-82	165.60	93.30	180.70	439.60	37.67	21.22	41.11
1982-83	178.70	99.40	197.20	475.30	37.60	20.91	41.49
1983-84	207.20	120.60	222.70	550.50	37.64	20.91	40.45
1984-85	234.90	113.90	284.10	632.90	37.11	18.00	44.89
VI Plan							
Average	183.80	112.14	208.94	504.88	36.41	22.21	41.38
1985-86	285.90	130.60	275.50	692.00	41.32	18.87	39.81
1986-87	337.80	158.30	414.40	910.50	37.10	17.39	45.51
1987-88	386.70	156.10	402.20	945.00	40.92	16.52	42.56
1988-89	442.70	153.30	428.70	1024.70	43.20	14.96	41.84
1989-90	524.80	198.60	572.60	1296.00	40.49	15.32	44.18
VII Plan							
Average	395.58	159.34	418.68	973.60	40.63	16.37	43.00
1990-91	668.80	201.10	694.10	1564.00	42.76	12.86	44.38

(Condt..)

1	2	3	4	5	6	7	8
1991-92	673.70	269.70	830.50	1774.00	37.98	15.21	46.82
1992-93	787.00	368.40	1008.80	2164.20	36.36	17.02	46.61
1993-94	916.10	451.90	1037.60	2405.60	38.07	18.79	43.13
VIII Plan	761.40	322.80	892.75	1976.95	38.51	16.33	45.16

Source : Government of Orissa, Statistical Abstract of Orissa, 1969, Orissa Budget (some facts and charts) 1977-78, Orissa Budget in Brief, 1985-86, and Orissa Budget in Brief, 1993-94.

GROWTH RATE : Column 3 = 14.5309 e0.o9133t, R^2= 0.9675.
Column 4 = 6.1476 e0.15624t, R^2= 0.9937.
Column 5 = 27.7733 e0.13105t, R^2= 0.9930.

AVERAGE AND MARGINAL TAX RATE

A more meaningful analysis of the changing tax-income ratio is made by relating the Average Tax Rate with the Marginal Tax Rate. The purpose of relating these two measures of the tax-income ratio is two fold.

First, the concept of marginal rate of taxation is useful in relation to a discussion on the appropriateness of the disposition of additional national income among several uses in any given country[3]. The marginal tax rate determines whether, and now fast, the tax ratio increases in the context of an increase in income over time. Here, it may be hypothesized that the higher per capita income, the easier it is to achieve a high marginal tax rate.

Second, the Average Tax Rate of the base period is likely to influence the marginal rate in so far as it is relatively easy with a given tax system to take out the same fraction from the incremental income as that from the original income base. Further, this will indicate the degree of variations in the tax revenue with respect to changes in the tax base.

The average tax rates have been calculated by following the formula :

$$= \frac{\text{Amount of taxes collected}}{\text{Size of the taxable base}}$$

The methodology may be described symbolically as follows :

If, RA_i and PB_i are the actual revenue and the potential base respectively for the jth tax in the state, then, the average tax rate is :

$$AR_i = \frac{RA_i}{PB_i}$$

On the other hand, for estimating the Marginal Tax Rate[4], the formula used in this case is :

$$= \frac{\text{Absolute change in Tax Revenue}}{\text{Absolute change in Tax Base}}$$

or, symbolically, we can put it :

$$MTR = \frac{\Delta\ T{\cdot}R}{\Delta\ T{\cdot}B}$$

where, MTR = Marginal Tax Rate,

Δ TR = change in tax revenue, and

Δ TB = change in tax base.

Table 5.3 is a refinement of Tables 5.1 and 5.2, and provides some further insight into the changing tax-income ratio over the planning period. The average and marginal tax rate are presented not only for the aggregate revenue but also for shared taxes and state's own tax revenues.

The findings based on Table 5.3 substantiate our earlier observation, which reveals that the average tax rate in case of state's own tax revenue has recorded a uniform pattern in all the plan periods covered by our study.

A closer perusal of Table 5.3 also suggests that for all practical purposes, there existed a shift in the pattern of tax revenue since the fiscal year 1961-62. And, by and large the Average Tax Rate seems to have registered a moderate increase for the state's own tax revenue and a sizable increase for the shared taxes. This is evident from the fact that, where the average tax rate of state's own tax, which was 4.27 percent in the year 1961-62 increased to only 5.87 percent in the year 1992-93, the average tax rate of shared taxes on the other hand, increased from 1.65 percent in the year 1961-62 to 7.50 percent in the year 1992-93.

Further, the disaggregation of the total tax revenues into those accruing to the state's own taxes and shared taxes respectively, clearly suggests that the bulk of the increase in the overall revenues has to be accounted for shared taxes. Of the 13.36 percent of the state income (column 2 of the table), taken away by the state and the union Governments in the year 1992-93, 7.51 percent was by the Union Government alone, and the rest 5.85 percent by the state Government. In other words, the Central Government has collected more than 56 percent of the total revenue, and the contribution of the state, itself, was only 44 percent.

TABLE 5.3

AVERAGE AND MARGINAL RATES OF TAXATION OVER THE PERIOD 1961-62 TO 1993-94, FOR THE STATE OF ORISSA.

(Rs. in crores)

Year	AVERAGE RATE ON			MARGINAL RATE ON		
	Total Tax Revenue	State's Own Tax	Shared Taxes	Total Tax Revenue	State's Own Tax Revenue	Shared Taxes
1	2	3	4	5	6	7
1961-62	4.27	2.62	1.65	7.14	3.13	4.02
1962-63	4.83	2.72	2.11	5.98	3.77	2.21
1963-64	4.99	2.87	2.12	3.07	3.57	- 0.50
1964-65	4.79	2.94	1.85	- 15.30	- 6.21	- 9.09

(Condt..)

1	2	3	4	5	6	7
1965-66	5.21	3.13	2.08	2.49	1.07	1.42
1966-67	4.70	2.74	1.95	4.61	3.12	1.49
1967-68	4.69	2.79	1.90	7.04	2.45	4.59
1968-69	4.88	2.76	2.12	9.64	2.97	6.68
1969-70	5.24	2.78	2.47	34.45	16.61	17.84
1970-71	6.05	3.16	2.89	94.02	16.74	77.28
1971-72	6.82	3.28	3.54	3.89	2.08	1.81
1972-73	6.26	3.05	3.21	2.12	0.73	1.40
1973-74	5.47	2.60	2.86	12.73	11.55	1.18
1974-75	5.77	2.98	2.79	47.38	26.49	20.90
1975-76	7.38	3.89	3.45	- 23.88	- 18.34	- 5.54
1976-77	8.63	4.77	3.85	1.70	0.69	1.00
1977-78	7.25	3.97	3.29	19.83	13.88	5.95
1978-79	7.85	4.44	3.42	244.21	40.65	203.56
1979-80	11.39	4.98	6.41	4.28	2.42	1.86
1980-81	9.45	4.28	5.97	11.36	6.98	4.38
1981-82	9.70	4.64	5.06	95.48	42.26	53.23
1982-83	10.40	4.96	5.48	4.43	2.34	2.09
1983-84	8.92	4.30	4.62	115.12	35.79	- 79.33
1984-85	10.95	4.95	5.99	4.65	5.59	- 0.94
1985-86	9.93	5.06	4.87	67.23	18.29	48.94
1986-87	12.67	5.69	6.98	17.06	22.73	-5.67
1987-88	12.82	6.29	6.54	6.83	4.64	2.19
1988-89	11.84	6.02	5.83	12.95	4.70	8.25
1989-90	12.05	5.76	6.29	12.50	6.78	5.72
1990-91	12.14	5.96	6.18	8.39	0.29	8.10
1991-92	11.65	5.22	6.43	54.68	21.25	33.43
1992-93	13.36	5.85	7.51	10.53	8.61	1.92
1993-94	13.07	6.13	6.94	13.07	6.13	6.94

NOTE : Calculation based on Tables 5.1 and 5.2.

Further, an attempt is made to work out the means and measures of Dispersion of the Average and Marginal Rate of taxation for the entire period covered by the study. The intention here is to ascertain the range of variation in these two tax rates over these years.

Figures about the degree of variation in these two tax rates are presented in Table 5.4.

It is observed from the foregoing table that, the coefficient of variation has changed. Simultaneously, in indicates that, the relative dispersion in average tax rate has remained more or less static. The table further exhibits that the marginal tax rate for the aggregate tax for the entire period covered by our study is 20.28 percent. This means that the state of Orissa, starting with a average tax rate of 5.837 percent in the mid 1970's had on average taxed away about 20 percent of the additional income.

Further, the results obtained from the above exercise suggest that during the particular period covered by the study, deliberate efforts on the part of the central Government in comparison to the state Government, which accounted for a substantial part of the variations in the marginal tax rate.

All these trends together with the increased claim in shared taxes at the first instance suggest that the increased tax burden in the state specially since 1979-80, has come mostly through the union Government.

Thus, from whatever angle, we look at the problem, it may be concluded that, the state has made meager tax efforts to mobilize adequate internal resources to meet its growing developmental needs.

While the following results based on the analysis of tax-income ratio reveal that, the state's own tax revenue mobilization efforts have not been commensurable as compared to other sources of revenue, viz.; shared taxes. The tax- income ratio does not reveal any significant characteristics of tax

TABLE 5.4
MEANS AND MEASURES OF DISPERSION OF AVERAGE AND MARGINAL TAX RATE, FOR 1961-62 TO 1993-94.

AVERAGE/ MARGINAL TAX RATE	MEAN DEVIATION	STANDARD OF VARIATION	COEFFICIENT
1	2	3	4
1. Average Tax Rate of total tax revenue for 1961-62 to 1979-80	5.8377	1.2273	0.2102
2. Average Tax Rate of total tax revenue for 1980-81 to 1993-94	11.3536	1.4056	0.1238
3. Average Tax Rate of state's own tax revenue for 1961-62 to 1979-80	3.2878	0.7265	0.2209
4. Average Tax Rate of state's own tax revenue for 1980-81 to 1993-94	5.3650	0.6551	0.1221
5. Average Tax Rate of shared taxes for 1961-62 to 1979-80	2.8421	1.06905	0.3761

(Condt..)

1	2	3	4
6. Average Tax Rate of shared taxes for 1980-81 to 1993-94	5.9921	0.8353	0.13940
7. Marginal Tax Rate of total tax revenue for 1961-62 to 1993-94	20.2860	52.5296	2.5899
8. Marginal Tax Rate of state's own tax revenue for 1961-62 to 1993-94	7.33848	14.10364	1.9218
9. Marginal Tax Rate of shared taxes for 1961-62 to 1993-94	12.9487	41.12096	3.1756

NOTE : Coefficient of variation is calculated by using Karl Pearson's formula of :

$$V = \frac{\sigma}{a} x\ 100$$

where, V = Coefficient of Variation, σ = Standard deviation and a = mean value of the series.

performance. The tax-income ratio neither give any idea about the nature of the tax base nor indicate the potential tax measures that may be utilized for augmenting revenues without unduly burdening the tax payers.

Secondly, the tax-income ratio does not tell about the relative weights or the extent of the contribution of individual taxes in the scheme of aggregate tax revenue. Since, these aspects are imperative in tax analysis, an attempt is made in the subsequent paragraph to study the desirability of use of different state's taxes and the relative contribution of each tax to the total revenue.

COMPOSITION OF STATE'S TAX REVENUE

With every effort at mobilizing additional resources through taxation, the importance of direct as well as indirect taxes has increased both in absolute and relative terms. In order to find out, how far these changes in the structure and yield of these taxes have remained consistent with the requirements of rapid and sustainable growth, we have attempted here an analysis of the trend in revenue yields from different taxes and also their relative place in the system of taxation.

As, it has been pointed out in the earlier paragraphs that it is intended to study the composition of tax revenues or the relative importance of specified individual taxes in terms of either the percentage of different taxes in the total tax revenue, or, the ratio of these taxes to Net State Domestic Product (NSDP), an attempt is made in this analysis to place more emphasis on the changes in the composition of tax revenue. The purpose is to focus on the background so as to provide the basis for the analytical discussion of the system in the latter chapters.

Table 5.5 provides more details on the composition of total tax revenues from 1961-62 to 1993-94. Figures in parenthesis in Table 5.5 represent the proportional contributions of different tax groups to the respective total tax revenues.

Based on at the elements of Table 5.5, we can infer that it is the indirect taxes that have been responsible for the major share in the increase in tax revenues of the Government over the years. While the total tax revenue have gone up by nearly one hundred sixteen-fold during 1961-62 to 1993-94, the direct tax revenues have gone only by fifty three times and indirect tax revenues by more than one hundred seventy three times. In absolute terms, over the period, while the indirect tax revenues have witnessed a tremendous increase of Rs. 1514.62 crores, the increase in direct taxes revenue is just of the order of Rs. 422.21 crores. Similar trend is observed even for a disaggregation of the total tax revenues into the parts accruing the state and the union respectively. While in the case of the state's direct taxes, the negative growth rate has been recorded from 1990's, in the case of the shared taxes, the decline in the share of direct taxes seems to have leveled off in recent years.

On the strength of the received theories of economic development, one would except that with the growth of the economy, the share of direct revenues in total revenues (and in total State/National income too) would show a steady increase, because with the increase in state and per capita incomes consequent on the expansion of economic activities, the scope for the expansion of direct taxes both in its horizontal as well as in its vertical directions would also be increasing. But, our findings based on the figures in the above table contradict to this generally held proposition. The reasons for the low significance of the state's direct taxes may be due to the existence of a highly predominant agricultural sector, which is not capable of the conditions warranted for successful use of direct taxation as an increasingly source of revenue to the state exchequer. In a most under developed state like Orissa, where more than 80 percent of the total population, directly or indirectly is engaged in the agricultural activities, a large part of the state income arises in the subsistence sector. It is estimated that upto one-half of the income originating in Orissa's agriculture consists of output retained by cultivators for own consumption. Therefore, sufficient income does not arise from market transactions, nor is it received or paid out in the form of money income. Clearly, when the major part of state product consists of such small retained incomes, in the agricultural sector it amounts to a virtual compression of the tax-base; and the persistent of tendency becomes a self defeating proposition, where tax revenue ceases to respond adequately to variations in the state product. As a result it has not been possible on the part of the state Government, to bring in better elasticity into the overall tax system through direct taxes. So, the self-propelling proposition, mentioned above, may well, be taken as one of the most plausible explanation for the rationalisation of the non-significant role of the direct taxes in the overall tax structure of the Orissan' economy.

Apart from the above, we may mention some other important factors that seem responsible for the declining importance of direct tax revenue of the state. They are : (a) the number of tax incentives and concessions or tax holidays that have been granted over the years for capital formation under the private sector in order to create a vibrant economic atmosphere, (b) the gradual disappearance of the agricultural income tax or, its negligible contribution to the total direct taxes there by giving rise to several leakages between the agricultural and industrial sectors, and (c) the existence of general poverty coupled with general deficiency in the purchasing power which has kept many people away from entering the direct tax net. All these trends noted above provide a dismal picture of state finance in case of Orssa.

On the other hand, the increasing reliance on indirect taxation in Orissa, however falls in line with the stand taken by Taxation Enquiry Commission and the planning commission, regarding the role and effectiveness of indirect taxation in India[5]. This in fact, reflects the views of Harberger[6], Lewis[7] and Wallich and Adler[8], where, they observed that direct taxes have a tendency to reduce the rate of savings more than would an indirect tax of equal revenue yield. Since, most of the underdeveloped economies face the problem of mobilization of savings to accelerate the pace of their economic development, they concluded that direct taxes on savings would have a deleterious effect on the rate of growth of these economies, which would probably be avoided, if the equivalent amount yielded by the tax could be raised through indirect levies. On the basis of this argument, we may be tempted to generalize the predominant role of indirect taxes in the Orissan tax system, which has its primary objective of resource mobilization for development needs.

TABLE 5.5
COMPOSITION OF THE TOTAL TAX REVENUES OF ORISSA (1961-62 TO 1993-94).

(Rs. in crores)

YEAR	DIRECT TAXES	INDIRECT TAXES	TOTAL TAXES	STATE TAXES	DIRECT TAXES	INDIRECT TAXES	SHARED TAXES	DIRECT TAXES	INDIRECT TAXES
1961-62	8.09	8.78	16.87	10.35	4.46	5.89	6.52	3.63	2.89
	(47.95)	(52.05)	(100.00)	(100.00)	(43.09)	(56.91)	(100.00)	(55.67)	(44.33)
1962-63	8.72	14.98	23.70	13.34	5.29	8.05	10.36	3.43	6.93
	(36.79)	(63.21)	(100.00)	(100.00)	(39.66)	(60.34)	(100.00)	(33.11)	(66.84)
1963-64	10.25	18.27	28.52	16.38	5.96	10.42	12.14	4.29	7.85
	(35.94)	(64.06)	(100.00)	(100.00)	(36.39)	(63.61)	(100.00)	(35.34)	(64.66)
1964-65	10.69	19.91	30.60	18.80	6.19	12.61	11.80	4.50	7.30
	(34.93)	(65.07)	(100.00)	(100.00)	(32.93)	(67.07)	(100.00)	(38.14)	(61.86)
1965-66	10.80	21.82	32.62	19.62	6.29	13.33	13.00	4.51	8.49
	(33.11)	(66.89)	(100.00)	(100.00)	(32.06)	(67.94)	(100.00)	(34.69)	(65.31)
1966-67	10.99	25.26	36.25	21.18	6.15	15.03	15.07	4.84	10.23
	(30.32)	(69.68)	(100.00)	(100.00)	(29.04)	(70.96)	(100.00)	(32.12)	(67.88)
1967-68	11.84	28.89	40.73	24.21	5.88	18.33	16.52	5.96	10.23
	(29.07)	(70.93)	(100.00)	(100.00)	(24.29)	(75.71)	(100.00)	(36.08)	(63.92)

1968-69	13.17 (28.60)	32.87 (71.38)	46.05 (100.00)	26.06 (100.00)	6.36 (24.41)	19.69 (75.76)	19.99 (100.00)	6.81 (34.07)	13.18 (65.93)
1969-70	17.88 (33.33)	35.77 (66.67)	53.65 (100.00)	28.40 (100.00)	6.75 (23.77)	21.65 (76.23)	25.25 (100.00)	11.13 (44.08)	14.12 (55.92)
1970-71	20.74 (32.55)	42.98 (67.46)	63.71 (100.00)	33.25 (100.00)	7.33 (22.05)	25.93 (77.98)	30.46 (100.00)	13.41 (44.02)	17.05 (55.98)
1971-72	25.38 (35.07)	46.97 (64.91)	72.36 (100.00)	34.79 (100.00)	8.14 (23.40)	26.64 (76.57)	37.57 (100.00)	17.24 (45.89)	20.33 (54.11)
1972-73	26.75 (32.61)	52.27 (63.73)	82.02 (100.00)	39.95 (100.00)	8.74 (21.88)	28.21 (70.61)	42.07 (100.00)	18.01 (42.81)	24.06 (57.19)
1973-74	29.30 (33.06)	59.32 (66.94)	88.62 (100.00)	42.21 (100.00)	9.46 (22.41)	32.75 (77.59)	46.41 (100.00)	19.84 (42.75)	26.57 (57.25)
1974-75	31.18 (31.93)	66.48 (68.07)	97.66 (100.00)	50.41 (100.00)	11.52 (22.85)	38.89 (77.15)	47.25 (100.00)	19.66 (41.61)	27.59 (58.39)
1975-76	41.92 (32.28)	87.95 (67.72)	129.88 (100.00)	68.42 (100.00)	14.22 (20.78)	54.19 (79.20)	61.46 (100.00)	27.70 (45.07)	33.76 (54.93)
1976-77	39.80 (27.26)	106.20 (72.74)	146.00 (100.00)	80.80 (100.00)	15.10 (18.69)	65.70 (81.31)	65.20 (100.00)	24.70 (37.88)	40.50 (62.12)

(Condt..)

YEAR	DIRECT TAXES	INDIRECT TAXES	TOTAL TAXES	STATE TAXES	DIRECT TAXES	INDIRECT TAXES	SHARED TAXES	DIRECT TAXES	INDIRECT TAXES
1977-78	42.30	110.80	153.10	83.70	16.70	67.00	69.40	25.60	43.80
	(27.63)	(72.37)	(100.00)	(100.00)	(19.95)	(80.05)	(100.00)	(36.89)	(63.11)
1978-79	46.00	128.10	174.10	98.40	19.20	79.20	75.70	26.80	48.90
	(26.42)	(73.58)	(100.00)	(100.00)	(19.51)	(80.49)	(100.00)	(35.40)	(64.60)
1979-80	52.60	203.80	256.40	112.10	20.20	91.90	144.30	32.40	111.90
	(20.51)	(79.49)	(100.00)	(100.00)	(18.02)	(81.98)	(100.00)	(22.45)	(77.55)
1980-81	62.30	230.30	292.60	132.60	24.60	108.00	160.00	37.70	122.30
	(21.29)	(78.71)	(100.00)	(100.00)	(18.55)	(81.45)	(100.00)	(23.56)	(76.44)
1981-82	70.20	276.10	346.30	165.60	32.50	133.10	180.70	37.70	143.00
	(20.27)	(79.73)	(100.00)	(100.00)	(19.63)	(80.37)	(100.00)	(20.86)	(79.14)
1982-83	77.00	298.80	375.90	178.70	34.60	144.00	197.20	42.40	154.80
	(20.48)	(79.49)	(100.00)	(100.00)	(19.36)	(80.58)	(100.00)	(21.50)	(78.50)
1983-84	86.40	343.50	429.90	207.20	42.50	164.70	222.70	43.90	178.80
	(20.10)	(79.90)	(100.00)	(100.00)	(20.51)	(79.49)	(100.00)	(19.71)	(80.29)
1984-85	99.40	419.60	519.00	234.90	43.60	191.30	284.10	55.80	228.30
	(19.15)	(80.85)	(100.00)	(100.00)	(18.56)	(81.44)	(100.00)	(19.64)	(80.36)

1985-86	136.10	425.30	561.40	285.90	58.50	227.40	275.50	77.60	197.90
	(24.24)	(75.76)	(100.00)	(100.00)	(20.46)	(79.54)	(100.00)	(28.17)	(71.83)
1986-87	163.80	588.40	752.20	337.80	74.90	262.90	414.40	88.90	325.50
	(21.78)	(78.22)	(100.00)	(100.00)	(22.17)	(77.83)	(100.00)	(21.45)	(78.55)
1987-88	195.30	593.60	788.90	386.70	87.00	299.70	402.20	108.30	293.90
	(24.76)	(75.24)	(100.00)	(100.00)	(22.50)	(77.50)	(100.00)	(26.93)	(73.07)
1988-89	213.90	657.50	871.40	442.70	99.20	343.50	428.70	114.70	314.00
	(24.55)	(75.45)	(100.00)	(100.00)	(22.41)	(77.59)	(100.00)	(26.76)	(73.24)
1989-90	309.10	788.30	1097.40	524.80	150.70	374.10	572.60	158.40	414.20
	(28.17)	(71.83)	(100.00)	(100.00)	(28.72)	(71.28)	(100.00)	(27.66)	(72.34)
1990-91	333.40	1029.50	1362.90	668.80	165.10	503.70	694.10	168.30	525.80
	(24.46)	(75.54)	(100.00)	(100.00)	(24.69)	(75.31)	(100.00)	(24.25)	(75.75)
1991-92	340.70	1163.50	1504.20	673.70	119.90	553.80	830.50	220.80	609.70
	(22.65)	(77.35)	(100.00)	(100.00)	(17.80)	(82.20)	(100.00)	(26.59)	(73.41)

(Condt..)

YEAR	DIRECT TAXES	INDIRECT TAXES	TOTAL TAXES	STATE TAXES	DIRECT TAXES	INDIRECT TAXES	SHARED TAXES	DIRECT TAXES	INDIRECT TAXES
1992-93	402.80	1393.00	1795.80	787.00	143.90	643.10	1008.80	258.90	749.90
	(22.43)	(77.57)	(100.00)	(100.00)	(18.28)	(81.72)	(100.00)	(25.66)	(74.34)
1993-94	430.30	1523.40	1953.70	916.10	162.20	753.90	1037.60	268.10	769.50
	(22.02)	(77.98)	(100.00)	(100.00)	(17.71)	(82.29)	(100.00)	(25.84)	(74.16)

Source: Government of Orissa, Statistical Abstract of Orissa 1969, Orissa Budget (some facts and chorts) 1977-78, Orissa Budget in Brief 1985-86, and Orissa Budget in Brief 1993-94. Figures in the parentheses indicates the proportion to the total.

NOTE : Growth Rate :

(i) Total Direct Taxes = $5.58661 e^{0.1285t}$, $R^2 = 0.9850$

(ii) Total Indirect Taxes = $9.3360 e^{0.15480}$, $R^2 = 0.9943$

(iii) State's own Direct Taxes = $2.7107 e^{0.1217t}$, $R^2 = 0.9597$

(iv) State's own Indirect Taxes = $5.9494 e^{0.14518}$, $R^2 = 0.9964$

(v) Shared Direct Taxes = $2.7364 e^{0.1356}$, $R^2 = 0.9815$

(vi) Shared Indirect Taxes = $3.4487 e^{0.1664}$, $R^2 = 0.9863$.

The changing compositional pattern of state's own tax revenue also primafacie suggests that, there existed a structural change in the fiscal year 1963-64. While the share of direct taxes in the state's own tax revenue during the period 1961-62 to 1963-64, has declined to the tune of just six percentage point, for the period 1963-64 to 1993-94, the recorded decline was almost three times of the decline observed from 1961-62 to 1963-64.

COMPOSITIONAL PATTERN OF STATE'S TAX REVENUE

It is evident from the above discussion that over the plan periods, a sizeable increase in tax revenues has been achieved through the horizontal and vertical integration of the structure of both direct and indirect taxes. The related issue that has to be spelt out in this connection is : were there any changes in the structure of state's own tax revenue, i.e.; in terms of the trend in revenue yields from various taxes and, what has been their relative contribution in the system of taxation over the last three decades covered by our study. Table 5.6 provides this information.

It is observed from Table 5.6 that the pattern of state's own taxes has changed significantly in relative terms, i.e.; there has been a tremendous increase in taxes on commodities and services (comprising taxes on electricity, state's sales tax and entertainment tax) at the expense of both agricultural taxes (comprising land revenue and agricultural income tax) and, taxes on property (comprising of Stamps and Registration), which we think is a product of time for the period taken as a whole. This trend is substantiated by the relative percentage contribution of these taxes to the state's own tax revenue. The percentage contribution of combined agricultural taxes and stamps and registration duty, which were of the order of 23.86 and 9.28 percent in the year 1961-62 fell consistently during the period under study and reached a level of 2.64 and 6.11 percent respectively in the

TABLE 5.6

RELATIVE CONTRIBUTIONS OF STATE'S OWN TAX AND SHARED TAXES IN TOTAL TAX REVENUES, 1961-62 TO 1993-94.

(Rs. in crores)

STATE'S OWN TAX REVENUE TAXES ON AGRICULTURAL TRANSACTION			TAXES ON PROP-		SHARED TAXES TAXES ON COMMODITIES AND SERVICES						LAND AND INCOME		ERTY & CAPITAL		
YEAR	LAND REVENUE	TAXES ON AGRICULTURAL INCOME	STAMPS & REGISTRATIONS	STATES EXCISE SUTY	TAXES ON VEHICLE	TAXES ON GOODS & PASSENGERS	ENTERTAIN-MENT TAX	TAXES ON ELECTRICITY	ENRAL SALES TAX	TOTAL OWN TAX	UNIOUN EXCISE DUTY	TAXES ON INCOME OTHER THAN AGRICULTURAL INCOME	ESTATE DUTY	TOTAL SHARED TAXES	TOTAL TAX REVENUE
(1)	(2)	(3)	(4)	(5)	(6)	(7)	(8)	(9)	(10)	(11)	(12)	(13)	(14)	(15)	(16)
1961-62	2.42 (14.34) *(23.38)	0.05 (0.30) *(0.48)	0.96 (5.69) *(9.28)	1.67 (9.90) *(16.14)	1.03 (6.11) *(9.95)	- - -	0.15 (0.89) *(1.45)	0.04 (0.24) *(0.39)	4.03 (23.89) *(38.94)	10.35 (61.35) *(100)	2.89 (17.13)	3.48 (20.63)	0.15 (0.89)	6.52 (38.65)	16.87 (100)
1962-63	2.79 (11.77) *(20.91)	0.11 (0.46) *(0.82)	1.10 (4.64) *(8.25)	1.81 (7.64) *(13.57)	1.29 (5.44) *(9.67)	- - -	0.22 (0.93) *(1.65)	0.52 (2.19) *(3.90)	5.50 (23.21) *(41.23)	13.34 (56.28) *(100)	6.93 (29.24)	3.28 (13.84)	0.15 (0.63)	10.36 (43.71)	23.70 (100)
1963-64	3.01 (10.55) *(18.38)	0.06 (0.21) *(0.37)	1.39 (4.87) *(8.49)	1.95 (6.84) *(11.90)	1.50 (5.26) *(9.16)	- - -	0.23 (0.81) *(1.40)	0.80 (2.81) *(4.85)	7.44 (26.09) *(45.42)	15.38 (57.43) *(100)	7.85 (27.52)	4.13 (14.48)	0.16 (0.56)	12.14 (42.57)	28.52 (100)
1964-65	2.99 (9.77) *(15.90)	0.06 (0.20) *(0.32)	1.49 (4.87) *(7.93)	2.13 (6.96) *(11.33)	1.65 (5.39) *(8.78)	- - -	0.26 (0.85) *(1.38)	1.23 (4.02) *(6.54)	8.99 (29.38) *(47.82)	18.80 (61.44) *(100)	7.30 (23.86)	4.25 (13.89)	0.25 (0.82)	11.80 (38.56)	30.60 (100)

1965-66	2.87	0.07	1.64	2.23	1.71	-	0.30	0.87	9.93	19.62	8.49	4.24	0.27	13.00	32.62
	(8.80)	(0.21)	(5.03)	(6.84)	(5.24)	-	(0.92)	(2.67)	(30.44)	(60.15)	(26.03)	(13.00)	(0.83)	(39.85)	(100)
	*(14.63)	*(0.36)	*(8.36)	*(11.37)	*(8.72)	-	*(1.53)	*(4.43)	*(50.61)	*(100)					
1966-67	2.51	0.07	1.70	2.45	1.87	-	0.39	1.10	11.09	21.18	10.23	4.68	0.16	15.07	36.25
	(6.92)	(0.19)	(4.69)	(6.76)	(5.16)	-	(1.08)	(3.03)	(30.59)	(58.43)	(28.22)	(12.91)	(0.44)	(41.57)	(100)
	*(11.85)	*(0.33)	*(8.03)	*(11.57)	*(8.83)	-	*(1.84)	*(5.19)	*(52.36)	*(100)					
1967-68	1.61	0.05	2.05	2.87	2.17	-	0.36	2.54	12.56	24.21	10.56	5.95	0.01	16.52	40.73
	(3.95)	(0.12)	(5.03)	(7.05)	(5.33)	-	(0.58)	(6.24)	(30.84)	(59.44)	(25.93)	(14.61)	(0.02)	(40.56)	(100)
	*(6.65)	*(0.21)	*(8.47)	*(11.85)	*(8.96)	-	*(1.49)	*(10.49)	*(51.88)	*(100)					
1968-69	1.58	0.07	2.13	4.16	2.59	-	0.39	2.08	13.06	26.06	13.18	6.64	0.17	19.99	46.05
	(3.43)	(0.15)	(4.63)	(9.03)	(5.62)	-	(0.85)	(4.52)	(28.26)	(56.59)	(28.62)	(14.42)	(0.37)	(43.41)	(100)
	*(6.06)	*(0.27)	*(8.17)	*(15.96)	*(9.94)	-	*(1.50)	*(7.98)	*(50.12)	*(100)					
1969-70	1.72	0.06	2.37	4.22	2.60	0.35	0.44	2.14	14.50	28.40	14.12	10.87	0.26	25.25	53.65
	(3.21)	(0.11)	(4.42)	(7.87)	(4.85)	(0.65)	(0.82)	(3.99)	(27.03)	(52.94)	(26.32)	(20.26)	(0.48)	(47.06)	(100)
	*(6.06)	*(0.21)	*(8.35)	*(14.86)	*(9.15)	*(1.23)	*(1.55)	*(7.54)	*(51.06)	*(100)					
1970-71	1.67	1.07	2.65	4.25	2.93	0.86	0.49	2.79	17.54	33.25	17.05	13.23	0.18	30.46	63.71
	(2.62)	(0.11)	(4.16)	(6.67)	(4.60)	(1.35)	(0.77)	(4.38)	(27.53)	(52.19)	(26.76)	(20.77)	(0.28)	(47.81)	(100)
	*(5.02)	*(0.21)	*(7.97)	*(12.78)	*(8.81)	*(2.59)	*(1.47)	*(8.39)	*(52.75)	*(100)					
1971-72	1.79	0.09	3.20	4.65	3.07	0.97	0.61	2.93	17.48	34.79	20.33	16.95	0.29	37.57	72.36
	(2.47)	(0.12)	(4.42)	(6.43)	(4.24)	(1.34)	(0.84)	(4.05)	(24.16)	(48.08)	(28.10)	(23.42)	(0.40)	(51.92)	(100)
	*(5.15)	*(0.26)	*(9.20)	*(13.37)	*(8.82)	*(2.79)	*(1.75)	*(8.42)	*(50.24)	*(100)					
1972-73	2.04	0.09	3.28	4.92	3.33	0.99	0.79	3.30	21.21	39.95	24.06	18.01	N.A	42.07	82.02
	(2.49)	(0.11)	(4.00)	(6.00)	(4.06)	(1.21)	(0.96)	(4.02)	(25.86)	(48.71)	(29.33)	(21.96)	-	(51.29)	(100)
	*(5.11)	*(0.23)	*(8.21)	*(12.32)	*(8.34)	*(2.48)	*(1.98)	*(8.26)	*(53.09)	*(100)					
1973-74	2.31	0.06	3.48	5.09	3.61	1.19	0.71	3.29	22.47	42.21	26.57	19.46	0.38	46.41	88.62
	(2.61)	(0.07)	(3.93)	(5.74)	(4.07)	(1.34)	(0.80)	(3.71)	(25.36)	(47.63)	(29.98)	(21.96)	(0.43)	(52.37)	(100)
	*(5.47)	*(0.14)	*(8.24)	*(12.06)	*(8.55)	*(2.82)	*(1.68)	*(7.79)	*(53.23)	*(100)					

(Condt..)

(1)	(2)	(3)	(4)	(5)	(6)	(7)	(8)	(9)	(10)	(11)	(12)	(13)	(14)	(15)	(16)
1974-75	2.43	0.06	4.37	5.51	4.66	1.47	1.15	3.45	27.31	50.41	27.59	19.12	0.54	47.25	97.66
	(2.49)	(0.06)	(4.47)	(5.64)	(4.77)	(1.51)	(1.18)	(3.53)	(27.96)	(51.62)	(28.25)	(19.58)	(0.55)	(48.38)	(100)
	*(4.82)	*(0.12)	*(8.67)	*(10.93)	*(9.24)	*(2.92)	*(2.28)	*(6.84)	*(54.18)	*(100)					
1975-76)	3.19	0.08	5.24	6.13	5.71	1.97	1.32	6.74	38.04	68.42	33.76	27.38	0.32	61.46	129.88
	(2.46)	(0.06)	(4.03)	(4.72)	(4.40)	(1.52)	(1.02)	(5.19)	(29.29)	(52.68)	(25.99)	(21.08)	(0.25)	(47.32)	(100)
	*(4.66)	*(0.12)	*(7.66)	*(8.96)	*(8.35)	*(2.88)	*(1.93)	*(9.85)	*(55.60)	*(100)					
1976-77	4.40	0.01	5.10	6.70	5.50	2.20	1.70	8.00	47.10	80.80	40.50	24.30	0.40	65.20	146.00
	(3.01)	(0.07)	(3.49)	(4.59)	(3.77)	(1.51)	(1.16)	(5.48)	(32.26)	(55.34)	(27.74)	(16.64)	(0.27)	(44.66)	(100)
	*(5.45)	*(0.12)	*(6.31)	*(8.29)	*(6.81)	*(2.72)	*(2.10)	*(9.90)	*(58.29)	*(100)					
1977-78	4.80	0.01	5.60	7.00	6.20	2.50	1.90	8.50	47.10	83.70	43.80	25.20	0.40	69.40	153.10
	(3.14)	(0.07)	(3.66)	(4.57)	(4.05)	(1.63)	(1.24)	(5.55)	(30.76)	(54.67)	(28.61)	(16.64)	(0.26)	(45.33)	(100)
	*(5.73)	*(0.12)	*(6.69)	*(8.36)	*(7.41)	*(2.99)	*(2.27)	*(10.16)	*(56.27)	*(100)					
1978-79	5.50	Neg.	6.60	7.20	7.01	2.80	2.10	11.90	55.20	98.40	48.90	26.40	0.40	75.70	174.10
	(3.16)	-	(3.79)	(4.14)	(4.08)	(1.61)	(1.21)	(6.84)	(31.71)	(56.52)	(28.09)	(15.16)	(0.23)	(43.48)	(100)
	*(5.59)	-	*(6.71)	*(7.32)	*(7.22)	*(2.85)	*(2.13)	*(12.09)	*(56.10)	*(100)					
1979-80	4.70	Neg.	7.20	7.80	8.30	2.80	2.80	12.60	65.90	112.10	111.90	32.30	0.10	144.30	256.40
	(1.83)	-	(2.81)	(3.04)	(3.24)	(1.09)	(1.09)	(4.91)	(25.70)	(43.72)	(43.64)	(12.60)	(0.04)	(56.28)	(100)
	*(4.19)	-	*(6.42)	*(6.96)	*(7.40)	*(2.50)	*(2.50)	*(11.24)	*(58.79)	*(100)					
1980-81	7.10	Neg.	7.80	9.20	9.70	2.30	3.00	16.90	76.60	132.60	122.30	37.50	0.20	160.00	292.60
	(2.43)	-	(2.67)	(3.14)	(3.32)	(0.79)	(1.03)	(5.78)	(26.18)	(45.32)	(41.80)	(12.82)	(0.07)	(54.68)	(100)
	*(5.35)	-	*(5.88)	*(6.94)	*(7.32)	*(1.73)	*(2.26)	*(12.75)	*(57.77)	*(100)					
1981-82	11.10	Neg.	9.30	11.00	12.10	1.30	3.60	22.90	94.30	165.60	143.00	38.00	-0.30	180.70	346.30
	(3.21)	-	(2.69)	(3.18)	(3.49)	(0.38)	(1.04)	(6.61)	(27.23)	(47.82)	(41.29)	(10.97)	- (0.09)	(52.18)	(100)
	*(6.70)	-	*(5.62)	*(6.64)	*(7.31)	*(0.79)	*(2.17)	*(13.83)	*(56.94)	*(100)					
1982-83	10.00	Neg.	10.80	13.10	13.80	1.70	3.90	23.30	102.10	178.70	154.80	42.30	0.10	197.20	375.90
	(2.66)	-	(2.87)	(3.48)	(3.67)	(0.45)	(1.04)	(6.20)	(27.16)	(47.54)	(41.18)	(11.25)	(0.03)	(52.46)	(100)
	*(5.60)	-	*(6.04)	*(7.33)	*(7.72)	*(0.95)	*(2.18)	*(13.04)	*(57.13)	*(100)					

1983-84	15.10 (3.51) *(7.29)	Neg. - -	12.50 (2.91) *(6.03)	15.50 (3.61) *(7.48)	14.90 (3.47) *(7.19)	3.70 (0.86) *(1.79)	4.00 (0.93) *(1.93)	27.50 (6.40) *(13.27)	114.00 (26.52) *(55.02)	270.00 (48.20) *(100)	178.80 (41.59)	43.80 (10.19)	0.10 (0.02)	222.70 (51.80)	429.90 (100)
1984-85	13.10 (2.52) *(5.58)	Neg. - -	14.30 (2.76) *(6.09)	18.70 (3.60) *(7.96)	62.20 (3.12) *(6.90)	9.80 (1.89) *(4.17)	4.10 (0.79) *(1.75)	32.50 (6.26) *(13.84)	126.20 (24.32) *(53.72)	234.90 (45.26) *(100)	220.30 (43.99)	56.10 (10.81)	-0.30 -0.06	284.10 (54.74)	519.00 (100)
1985-86	15.90 (2.83) *(5.56)	Neg. - -	17.30 (3.08) *(6.05)	21.60 (3.85) *(7.56)	25.30 (4.51) *(8.85)	2.50 (0.45) *(0.87)	5.10 (0.91) *(1.78)	49.80 (8.89) *(17.45)	148.40 (26.43) *(51.91)	285.90 (50.93) *(100)	197.90 (35.25)	77.60 (13.82)	N.A. -	275.50 (49.07)	561.40 (100)
1986-87	20.80 (2.77) *(6.16)	Neg. - -	20.30 (2.70) *(6.01)	22.80 (3.03) *(6.75)	31.80 (4.23) *(9.41)	0.20 (0.03) *(0.06)	5.50 (0.73) *(1.63)	60.20 (8.00) *(17.82)	176.20 (23.42) *(52.16)	337.80 (44.91) *(100)	325.50 (43.27)	90.80 (12.07)	0.10 (0.01)	414.40 (55.09)	752.20 (100)
1987-88	30.20 (3.83) *(7.81)	Neg. - -	22.20 (2.81) *(5.74)	26.50 (3.36) *(6.85)	34.60 (4.39) *(8.95)	0.70 (0.09) *(0.18)	5.40 (0.68) *(1.40)	61.10 (7.74) *(15.80)	206.00 (26.11) *(53.27)	386.70 (49.02) *(100)	293.80 (37.25)	108.30 (13.73)	Neg. -	402.20 (50.98)	788.90 (100)
1988-89	35.60 (4.09) *(8.04)	Neg. - -	25.60 (2.94) *(5.78)	31.00 (3.56) *(7.00)	38.00 (4.36) *(8.58)	0.20 (0.02) *(0.05)	5.50 (0.63) *(1.24)	68.40 (7.85) *(15.45)	238.30 (27.35) *(53.83)	442.70 (50.80) *(100)	314.00 (36.03)	114.80 (13.17)	-0.10 -0.01	428.70 (49.20)	871.40 (100)
1989-90	78.90 (7.91) *(15.03)	Neg. - -	27.90 (2.54) *(5.32)	38.30 (3.49) *(7.30)	43.90 (4.00) *(8.37)	0.10 (0.01) *(0.02)	5.10 (0.46) *(0.97)	33.40 (3.04) *(6.36)	297.20 (27.08) *(56.63)	524.80 (47.82) *(100)	414.20 (37.74)	158.40 (14.43)	N.A. -	572.60 (52.18)	1097.40 (100)
1990-91	81.90 (6.01) *(12.25)	Neg. - -	30.90 (2.27) *(4.62)	45.60 (3.35) *(6.82)	52.30 (3.84) *(7.82)	0.10 (0.01) *(0.01)	4.60 (0.34) *(0.69)	98.90 (7.26) *(14.79)	354.60 (26.02) *(53.02)	668.80 (49.07) *(100)	525.80 (38.58)	168.30 (12.35)	N.A. -	694.10 (50.93)	1362.90 (100)
1991-92	24.80 (1.65) *(3.68)	Neg. - -	35.40 (2.35) *(5.25)	55.10 (3.66) *(8.18)	59.70 (3.92) *(8.86)	Neg. - -	5.00 (0.33) *(0.74)	99.50 (6.61) *(14.77)	394.20 (26.21) *(58.51)	673.70 (44.79) *(100)	609.70 (40.53)	220.80 (14.68)	N.A. -	830.50 (52.21)	1504.20 (100)

(Condt..)

(1)	(2)	(3)	(4)	(5)	(6)	(7)	(8)	(9)	(10)	(11)	(12)	(13)	(14)	(15)	(16)
1992-93	25.90	Neg.	44.50	65.00	73.50	Neg.	5.00	103.10	470.00	787.00	749.90	258.90	N.A.	1008.80	1795.80
	(1.44)	-	(2.48)	(3.62)	(4.09)	-	(0.28)	(5.74)	(26.17)	(43.82)	(41.76)	(14.42)	-	(56.18)	(100)
	*(3.29)	-	*(5.65)	*(8.26)	*(9.34)	-	*(0.64)	*(13.10)	*(59.72)	*(100)					
1993-94	24.20	Neg.	56.00	76.80	82.00	Neg.	5.00	116.20	555.30	916.10	769.50	268.10	N.A.	1037.60	1953.70
	(1.24)	-	(2.87)	(3.93)	(4.20)	-	(0.26)	(5.95)	(28.42)	(46.89)	(39.39)	(13.72)	-	(53.11)	(100)
	*(2.64)	-	*(6.11)	*(8.38)	*(8.95)	-	*(0.55)	*(12.68)	*(60.62)	*(100)					

Source : Government of Orissa, Statistical Abstract of Orissa (1969), Orissa Budget (1977-78), (1985-86), and, (1993-94).

Note : (i) Figures in Parenthesis indicate the proportion to total

(ii) Figures in Parenthesis with star-mark indicate the proportion to state own tax-revenue

(iii) N.A. = Not Available (iv) Neg. = Negligible

Growth Rate : Column 2 = 1.0081 e0.1095t, R2 = 0.0052

Column 3 = 199.5045 e0.12087t, R2 = 0.0052

Column 4 = 0.82003 e0.12087t, R2 = 0.9939

Column 5 = 1.25155 e0.1142t, R2 = 0.9750

Column 6 = 0.7865 e0.1351t, R2 = 0.9846

Column 7 = 9.7184 e-0.0015t, R2 = 0.0912

Column 8 = 0.18181 e0.1210t, R2 = 0.9393

Column 9 = 0.3381 e0.1880t, R2 = 0.93010

Column 10 = 4.1248 e0.1458t, R2 = 0.9953

Column 11 = 8.7864 e0.13867t R2 = 0.9939

Column 12 = 3.4487 e0.16644t, R2 = 0.9863

Column 13 = 2.6278 e0.13726t, R2 = 0.9818

Column 14 = 260.0185 e-0.00135t, R2 = 0.0643

Column 15 = 6.14765 e0.15624t R2 = 0.9937

Column 16 = 14.9067 e0.14699t, R2 = 0.9958

year, 1993-94. This trend conforms the esstablished theoretical and empirically hypothesis: with the gradual commercialization and modernization of an economy, it would be possible for an economy in transition to shift from agricultural and property taxes to taxes on commodities and services. The noteworthy feature however is the stagnant or non-existence of agricultural taxes, both in absolute and in proportional terms. Against the 107 percentage points increase of the agricultural sector's contribution to state income during the period 1961-62 to 1993-94, the contribution of taxes on agriculture to total tax revenues has increased by just 11 percentage points.

Taking next, the changes in the composition of taxes on commodities and services during the period 1961-62 to 1993-94 on the resource mobilisation front, the enormous growth in revenues from these taxes has certainly to be attributed to state's sales tax. The percentage contribution of sales tax to state's own tax revenue which was only 38.94 percent in the year 1961-62, has enormously increased to 60.62 percent in the year 1993-94. Its growth in absolute revenues however, is commendable especially since the fiscal year 1981-82. The major factors that have contributed to the growth of sales taxation to its predominant position are : (a) the unprecedented extension of sales taxation along with the expansion of tax base and, (b) frequent upward revision of its rate from time to time. The greatest relative decline has taken place in revenue from state's excise duty, from 16.14 percent of state's own tax revenue in 1961-62 to 8.38 percent in 1993-94. The explanation to the steep fall in state's excise lies either due to several tax leakages or due to the Government's restrictions on the consumption of nacrotics and liquor. Further, it can be inferred that taxes on electricity had played a major role in state's tax revenues. Gross receipts under this, as observed from the foregoing table 4.6, have increased from 0.39 percent of state's own tax revenue in 1961-62 to 12.68 percent in 1993-94. The greatest improvement in the relative significance of taxes on electricity from 1975-76, reflects the rationalization of electricity duty in the recent years' budgets. The relative percentage contribution of all other state's taxes, viz.; entertainment tax, taxes on vehicle, and taxes on goods and passengers has accounted for a relatively stable proportion of state's own taxes over the last three decades covered by our study.

Turning to the shared taxes, we observed the similar pattern as exhibited by the state's own tax revenue. The state's share of union excise duty in the shared taxes pool shows an increasing trend, from 44.33 percent in the year 1961-62 to 74.16 percent in the year 1993-94, where as, the percentage share of taxes on income other than agricultural income and Estate duty in the gross shared taxes shows a declining trend through out the period under study.

A noteworthy feature of state's taxation as revealed by the above table is that the tremendous increase in share of central taxes in total tax revenue has out paced the relative contribution of state's own tax revenue to the total tax revenue of the state. The percentage contribution of shared taxes to the total tax revenue of state has tremendously increased from 38.65 percent in the year 1961-62 to 53.11 percent in the year 1993-94. This continual out pacing of state's own tax revenue by the shared taxes gets substantiated by the figures presented in Table 5.6, where as the overall percentage contribution of state's own individual taxes to the total tax revenue exhibits a declining trend throughout. The increasing reliance of the state on the share of union taxes might partly be due to the better built-in-flexibility that the central government has brought into the shared taxes.

However, the trend that we observe from the compositional pattern of state's taxes is not at all warranted from the point of view of a sound fiscal practice. The reverse would have been commendable in the context of state's relative degree of self-reliance as regards to the mobilization of adequate resources for its own developmental needs. To substantiate our argument, we have also worked out the ratio of specified taxes to the state income.

RATIO OF INDIVIDUAL TAXES TO STATE INCOME

The degree of success in resource mobilization by the Government can be judged from the improvement in the proportion of state income or, Net State Domestic Product taken away as taxes. Further, the percentages of different sources of revenue to state income is usually used to study shifts in tax structure. With these ends in mind, an attempt is made to relate the specified taxes to state income and, Table 5.7 provides the relevant informations.

Table 5.7 exhibits the fact, that the share of total tax revenue to Net State Domestic Product has increased from 4.27 percent in the year 1961-62 to 13.07 percent in 1993-94. As already stated, land revenue is a declining source of revenue. From 0.61 percent of state income in 1961-62, it declined to 0.16 percent in the year 1993-94. Receipts from state excise duty, which was 0.42 percent in 1961-62 has slightly increased to 0.51 percent in 1993-94. It was again sales tax, where the increased was very large. From, 1.02 percent of state income in 1961-62, it increased to 3.72 percent in 1993-94. Stamps duty and motor vehicle tax also showed an increasing trend during the period under study. Whereas in 1961-62, they constituted only 0.24 and 0.26 percent of state income respectively, this proportion almost doubled to 0.37 and 0.55 percent in the year 1993-94. In case of other taxes and duties, no consistent trend emerges, though as a proportion of state income, they appeared to be falling over the period under study. Based on our findings, we may draw the following inferences :

(i) If we Judge from the angle of ratio of state's own taxes to the state income, then its observed that out of the 5.85 percent of state income mobilised through taxation in the year 1992-93, near about 3.50 percent has to be

Table 5.7
Tax Revenue As Percentage On Net State Domestic Product In Orissa, 1961-62 To 1993-94

Yeras	Total Tax Revenue	Total Direct Taxes	Total Indirect Taxes	Shared Taxes	State's Own Taxes	Land Revenue	Agri. Income Tax	Stamps Duty	State Excise	Vehicle Tax	Taxes on Electricty	Taxes on Goods and Pass engers	Enter tainment Tax	Sales Tax	Union Excise	Taxes on Income other than Agri.	Estate Duty
(1)	(2)	(3)	(4)	(5)	(6)	(7)	(8)	(9)	(10)	(11)	(12)	(13)	(14)	(15)	(16)	(17)	(18)
1961-62	4.27	2.05	2.22	1.65	2.62	0.61	0.01	0.24	0.42	0.26	0.01	...	0.04	1.02	0.73	0.88	0.04
1962-63	4.83	1.78	3.05	2.11	2.72	0.57	0.02	0.22	0.37	0.26	0.11	...	0.04	1.12	1.41	0.67	0.03
1963-64	4.99	1.79	3.20	2.12	2.87	0.53	0.01	0.24	0.34	0.26	0.14	...	0.04	1.30	1.37	0.72	0.03
1964-65	4.79	1.67	3.12	1.85	2.94	0.47	0.01	023	0.33	0.26	0.19	...	0.04	1.41	1.14	0.66	0.04
1965-66	5.21	1.73	3.49	2.08	3.13	0.46	0.01	0.26	0.36	0.27	0.14	...	0.05	1.59	1.36	0.68	0.04
1966-67	4.70	1.42	3.27	1.95	2.74	0.33	0.01	0.22	0.32	0.24	0.14	...	0.05	1.44	1.33	0.61	0.02
1967-68	4.69	1.36	3.33	1.90	2.79	0.19	0.01	0.24	0.33	0.25	0.29	...	0.04	1.45	1.22	0.68	...
1968-69	4.88	1.39	3.48	2.12	2.76	0.17	0.01	0.23	0.44	0.27	0.22	...	0.04	1.38	1.40	0.70	0.02
1969-70	5.24	1.75	3.50	2.47	2.78	0.17	0.01	0.23	0.41	0.25	0.21	0.03	0.04	1.42	1.38	1.06	0.03

1970-71	6.05	1.97	4.08	2.89	3.16	0.16	0.01	0.25	0.40	0.28	0.27	0.08	0.05	1.67	1.62	1.26	0.02
1971-72	6.82	2.39	4.42	3.54	3.28	0.17	0.01	0.30	0.44	0.29	0.28	0.09	0.06	1.65	1.92	1.60	0.03
1972-73	6.26	2.04	3.99	3.21	3.05	0.16	0.01	0.25	0.38	0.25	0.25	0.08	0.06	1.62	1.84	1.37	...
1973-74	5.47	1.81	3.66	2.86	2.60	0.14	...	0.21	0.31	0.22	0.20	0.07	0.04	1.39	1.64	1.20	0.02
1974-75	5.77	1.84	3.93	2.79	2.98	0.14	...	0.26	0.33	0.28	0.20	0.09	0.07	1.61	1.63	1.13	0.03
1975-76	7.38	2.38	5.00	3.45	3.89	0.18	...	0.30	0.35	0.32	0.38	0.11	0.08	2.16	1.92	1.56	0.02
1976-77	8.63	2.35	6.28	3.85	4.77	0.26	0.01	0.30	0.40	0.33	0.47	0.13	0.10	2.78	2.39	1.44	0.02
1977-78	7.25	2.00	5.25	3.29	3.92	0.23	...	0.27	0.33	0.29	0.40	0.12	0.09	2.23	2.08	1.19	0.02
1978-79	7.85	2.08	5.78	3.42	4.44	0.25	...	0.30	0.32	0.32	0.53	0.13	0.09	2.49	2.21	1.19	0.02
1979-80	11.39	2.34	9.06	6.41	4.98	0.21	...	0.32	0.35	0.37	0.56	0.12	0.12	2.93	4.97	1.44	...
1980-81	9.45	2.01	7.44	5.17	4.28	0.23	...	0.25	0.30	0.31	0.55	0.07	0.10	2.47	3.95	1.21	0.01
1981-82	9.70	1.97	7.74	5.06	4.64	0.31	...	0.26	0.31	0.34	0.64	0.04	0.10	2.64	4.01	1.06	- 0.01
1982-83	10.44	2.14	8.30	5.48	4.96	0.28	...	0.30	0.36	0.38	0.65	0.05	0.11	2.84	4.30	1.18	...
1983-84	8.92	1.79	7.13	4.62	4.30	0.31	...	0.26	0.32	0.31	0.57	0.08	0.08	2.37	3.71	0.91	...
1984-85	10.95	2.10	8.85	5.99	4.95	0.28	...	0.30	0.39	0.34	0.69	0.21	0.09	2.66	4.82	1.18	- 0.01
1985-86	9.93	2.41	7.52	4.87	5.06	0.28	...	0.31	0.38	0.45	0.88	0.04	0.09	2.63	3.50	1.37	...
1986-87	12.67	2.76	9.91	6.98	5.69	0.35	...	0.34	0.38	0.54	1.01	...	0.09	2.97	5.48	1.53	...
1987-88	12.82	3.17	9.65	6.54	6.29	0.49	...	0.36	0.43	0.56	0.99	0.01	0.09	3.35	4.78	1.76	...

(Condt..)

(1)	(2)	(3)	(4)	(5)	(6)	(7)	(8)	(9)	(10)	(11)	(12)	(13)	(14)	(15)	(16)	(17)	(18)
1988-89	11.84	2.91	8.93	5.83	6.02	0.48	...	0.35	0.42	0.52	0.93	...	0.07	3.24	4.27	1.56	...
1989-90	12.05	3.39	8.66	6.29	5.76	0.87	...	0.31	0.42	0.48	0.37	...	0.06	3.26	4.55	1.74	...
1990-91	12.14	2.97	9.17	6.18	5.96	0.73	...	0.28	0.41	0.47	0.88	...	0.04	3.16	4.68	1.50	...
1991-92	11.65	2.64	9.01	6.43	5.22	0.19	...	0.27	0.43	0.46	0.77	...	0.04	3.05	4.72	1.71	...
1992-93	13.36	3.00	10.36	7.50	5.85	0.19	...	0.33	0.48	0.55	0.77	...	0.04	3.50	5.58	1.93	...
1993-94	13.07	2.88	10.19	6.94	6.13	0.16	...	0.37	0.51	0.55	0.78	...	0.03	3.72	5.15	1.79	...

NOTE : Calculations are based on Table 5.1 and 5.5

accounted for state's sales tax alone. The overall incidence of sales tax has more than tripled from 1.02 percent in 1961-62 to 3.50 percent in 1992-93. This clearly shows that state's sales tax has emerged as one of the most vibrant sources of state's own tax revenue over the years. Whereas, the rest 2.35 percent of the state income is attributed to all other state's own taxes (comprising Agricultural taxes stamps and registration, taxes on vehicle, state's excise duty, Entertainment tax and Electricity duty). Thus, from the point of view of productivity, the performances of all these state's taxes are quite discoveraging and;

(ii) A closer observation of the over time, behaviour of this ratio discloses that during the entire period of the study, the overall incidence of indirect taxes has increased near about five times from 2.22 percent in 1961-62 to 10.19 percent in the year 1993-94. Further, it is to be noted that the relative importance of different taxes, however, has not changed much, when they are related to state income.

So, in the absence of any additional measures to mobilise adequate revenue, the state of Orissa remains far away from the degree of financial self-reliance, whose dependence on federal transfers constitute more than fifty five percent of the total fiscal resources of the state. The in capacity of the government to mobilize adequate resources to meet its ever increasing demand for public services has no doubt resulted in a growing and widening gap between the state's own financial resources and its expenditure requirements. This has generated a need for increasing transfers of funds from the centre to the state. Keeping these broad trends in view, the quantitative implications of federal transfer to Orissa are examined in the subsequent section of this chapter.

SECTION - II

In this section, an attempt has been made to examine the size and composition of all types of federal transfers to the state in order to determine their relative magnitude in the overall fiscal scenerio of the state.

TRENDS AND PATTERNS OF FEDERAL TRANSFERS

The trends in the composition of federal transfers with reference to its main components, namely, (i) tax devolution, that is state's share of the central taxes determined on the basis of recommendations of the Finance Commission, (ii) grants-in-aid of different categories, and, (iii) central loans are examined in the following paragraphs.

The present pattern of state finance in Orissa as in in a federal set up has been shaped and tuned to the spirit of fiscal federalism embodied in the constitution.

Over the time, the principle of fiscal federalism in India has under gone vast changes. After independence, the fiscal deficiency approach was embodied in the constitution more rigidly. As the Report of Taxation Enquiry Commission puts it :

"The Constitution of India closely follows the pattern of division of tax powers between the centre and the states established by the Government of India Act, 1935. Under the quasi-federal character of our constitution, failary wide powers are vested in the states, but residual powers of taxation belong to the union".[9]

The emergence of the planning commission as a central planning authority determining the size of plan grants to the state has resulted in the increase of the centre's financial control over the states. In the light of this intensified adherence to the principle of fiscal deficiency, Orissa's state finance has shown a distinct trend where, its dependence on federal transfers has been rapidly growing. With this background, an attempt is made in the following paragraphs to ascertain the compositional magnitude of the total central transfers in the overall state finances.

Table 5.8 gives a picture of the total resources transferred from the union to the state during the period 1961-62 to 1993-94. The union transfers representing 52.18 percent of the total state's expenditure in the Third Five year plan period rose sharply to 57.45 percent in the Fourth Five Year plan period, further increased to 61.75 percent in the Annual Plan periods of 1978-79 to 1979-80. In the Sixth Five Year plan, it recorded a decline to 41.68 percent, but the figures for Eighth plan period indicates a sharp rise to 48.03 percent. In the Seventh plan, Fifth plan and, the Annual plans of 1966-67 to 1968-69, the figures have stabilized around this percentage. Consequently, this level can be hypothesized as the probable level of dependence of the state on union transfers in the coming years also.

A closer examination of Table 5.8 also discloses that the funds made available to the state through the statutory transfers amount to only 43.99 percent of the total union allocation. The balance of 56.01 percent is in the form of non-statutory transfers made either as grants or loans on adhoc basis through the Planning Commission.

The foregone table clearly reveals the declining significance of statutory grants, over a perid of time. The important factors that have contributed to the declining effectiveness of the finance commission in determining the nature and quantum of financial assistance to the state by the union could be found in the character of the central planning process that the economy has adopted.[10] But, on the other hand, the increasing dependence of the state Government on the non-statutory grants (although this percentage shows a declining trend, but with comparison to the statutory grants) would not prove to be a viable proposition de rose for maintaining the financial autonomy of the state. This clearly shows the over dependence of the state Government on the central grants and contributions, which may not be branded as a healthy tradition.

TABLE 5.8
TRANSFER OF FINANCIAL RESOURCES FROM THE UNION TO THE STATE, 1961-62 TO 1993-94.

(Rs. in crores)

	THIRD FIVE YEAR PLAN (1961-62 TO 1965-66)	ANNUAL PLANS (1966-67 TO 1968-69)	FOURTH FIVE YEAR PLAN (1969-70 TO 1973-74)	FIFTH FIVE YEAR PLAN (1974-75 TO 1977-78) 1979-80)	ANNUAL PLANS (1978-79) To	SIXTH FIVE YEAR PLAN (1980-81 TO 1984-85)	SEVENTH FIVE YEAR PLAN (1985-86 TO 1989-90	EIGHTH FIVE YEAR PLAN 1990-91 TO 1993-94 (UPTO FOURTH YEAR)
	1	2	3	4	5	6	7	8
1. SHARE OF DIVISIBLE TAXES AND DUTIES	53.82 (16.92)	51.58 (16.51)	181.76 (23.25)	243.31 (27.25)	220.00 (28.66)	1044.70 (35.22)	2093.40 (38.43)	3571.00 (39.25)
2. GRANTS-IN-AID	93.63 (29.44)	123.33 (39.46)	216.50 (27.69)	407.34 (45.63)	328.40 (42.78)	1106.90 (37.31)	1885.30 (34.61)	3312.10 (36.40)
2. (a) STATUTORY GRANTS (WITHIN THE PURVIEW OF FINANCE COMMISSION)	54.25 (17.05)	94.54 (30.25)	111.99 (14.32)	249.58 (27.96)	119.70 (15.59)	114.70 (3.87)	197.00 (3.62)	431.90 (4.75)

(Condt..)

		1	2	3	4	5	6	7	8
2.	(b) OTHER GRANTS (WITHIN THE PURVIEW OF PLANNING COMMISSION AND FINANCE MINISTRY)	39.38 (12.38)	28.79 (9.21)	104.51 (13.37)	157.76 (17.67)	208.70 (27.19)	992.20 (33.45)	1688.30 (30.99)	2880.20 (31.66)
3.	LOANS	170.60 (53.64)	137.59 (44.03)	383.58 (49.06)	242.13 (27.12)	219.30 (28.57)	814.80 (27.47)	1468.00 (26.95)	2215.00 (24.35)
4.	TOTAL RESOURCES TRANSFERRED	318.05 (100)	312.50 (100)	781.84 (100)	892.78 (100)	767.70 (100)	2966.40 (100)	5446.70 (100)	9098.10 (100)
5.	TOTAL STATUTORY TRANSFERS (1+2a)	108.07 (33.98)	146.12 (46.76)	293.75 (37.57)	492.89 (55.21)	339.70 (44.25)	1159.40 (39.08)	2290.40 (42.05)	4002.90 (43.99)
6.	TOTAL NON-STATUTORY TRANSFERS	209.98 (66.02)	166.38 (53.24)	488.09 (62.43)	399.89 (44.79)	428.00 (55.75)	1807.00 (60.92)	3156.30 (57.95)	5095.20 (56.01)

(Condt..)

	1	2	3	4	5	6	7	8
7. STATE'S TOTAL OWN RESOURCES (TAX & NON-TAX)	184.90	157.40	362.72	506.88	342.30	1479.70	2774.80	4336.80
8. AGGREGATE STATE'S EXPENDITURE	609.52	652.61	1360.99	2015.13	1243.30	7116.70	12087.50	18940.50
9. TOTAL RESOURCE TRANS- FERRED TO AGGREGATE STATE'S EXPENDITURES	52.18	47.88	57.45	44.30	61.75	41.68	45.06	48.03
10. STATES OWN SOURCES OF REVENUE TO AGGREGATE STATE'S EXPENDITURES	30.34	24.12	26.65	25.15	27.53	20.79	22.96	22.89

Source : Government of Orissa, Statistical Abstract of Orissa, 1969, Orissa Budget papers for, 1977-78, 1985-86, 1993-94.

NOTE : Figures in the parenthesis indicate the proportions to the total.

Further, Table 5.8 reveals that the state's share of divisible taxes and duties has gone up both in absolute and relative tern, from Rs. 53.82 crores during the of third Five Year plan to Rs. 3571 crores in the Eighth Five Year plan periods. The percentage share of divisible taxes to the total resources transferred, which was 16.92 percent in the Third Five Year plan has gone up to 39.25 percent in the Eighth Five Year plan periods. And, it showed a steady increase all through. This trend no doubt has created a repercussion effect on the growth and sustenance of the taxation efforts of the state in recent times. Rather, it has dampened the tax effort of the state.

Further, if the relative importance of federal transfer in the over all composition of state finance can be taken as a standard yard-stick to measure the relative degree of self-reliance of the State, then the findings of the foregoing table strengthen the conclusion drawn earlier that Orissa's degree of self-reliance is remarkably low. This may be substantiated by Orissa's exceptionally high dependence on grants, the high and increasing share of tax devolution, and the relatively small share of own taxes and non-tax revenue in the overall resource mobilization effort of the state.

CONCLUDING REMARKS

To sum up, we may say that there are two major trends, which emerges from our overall findings in this chapter.

First, judged from the angle of state's own resource mobilisation, a progressive system of direct taxes on agricultural land, agricultural income and Estate Duty, in the hope as to make available to the state as much of revenue from these sources as can be collected through them, against the back drop of the constraints of the low amount of per capita income and wealth and the highly unequal nature of their distribution in a predominantly agrarian structure of the Orissan economy, had already been put on the statute book in all the plan periods. This is supported by the evidence that, the contribution of the total agricultural taxes to the state's own tax revenue has remained almost static during the last two decades of 1970-71 to 1993-94. Thus, the system of agricultural taxation appears to have designed for a static and subsistence Agriculture. That seems to be the plausible reason, why the system has remained almost inelastic with respect to changes in prices and production over the years. An analysis of the revenues from this source and the relevant proxy bases, viz.; agricultural income and the level of agricultural production, indicates a considerable scope for raising revenue from these categories of taxes. In other words, its rate of growth was estimated to be much lower than that of the relevant bases such as agricultural income and agricultural production. As the revenue requirements of the state are duly high, this source needs to be adequately tapped.

However, against the background of the reluctance of the state Government not only to increase the rates of these taxes, but even to continue to keep these taxes on the statute book at the existing rates, and the land reform measures of imposing ceilings on the ownership of agricultural land which in trun has given rise to benani holdings it is doubtful, whether the amount of revenues which could be mobilized through these agricultural taxes would be commensurate with the cost of administering these taxes.

But, the truth remains that, with the secular upward trend in prices and consequent heightened income structure, the inelastic agricultural taxes are losing importance as an important source of public revenue in the state.

Secondly, in the process of gradual commercialization of the economy, there has been a continual shift from the taxes on agricultural land, income and property to the taxes on commodities and services. The primary consideration in the wider coverage and increased rate of these taxes during the plan periods has been the motive to obtain the ever-mounting resources for developmental purposes. At the same time, these taxes have been expected to impose certain amount of restraints on increase in consumption thereby releasing additional resources for developmental needs. But, the continual outpacing of the state's own tax revenue by the shared taxes raises serious doubt about the relative tax-effort of the state on the one hand, and indicates the relative inelastic nature of state's taxes (or the productivity of state's own taxes) to those of the shared taxes, on the other hand.

There is thus substantial evidence to support that to a large extent, the development of the present day tax system in Orissa, has been done through a patch work adjustment process. Hence a reappraisal of the built-in-responsiveness in terms of elasticity and buoyancy of the constituent tax instruments has much current significance. This besides being essential for arriving at a proper assessment of each one of the taxes' revenue yielding potential would help in identifying factors responsible for the observed anomaly, would enable us to locate the areas, where scope for further taxation lies and indicate where more improvement of the tax administration could be of considerable usefulness. An attempt therefore is made to look into these intrinsic problems in the next chapter.

NOTES AND REFERENCES

1. Douglas, M.; "Taxable Capacity and British and Canadian Experience", on Limits of Taxable Capacity (Princeton, N.J., Tax Institute, Inc. 1953) p. 31.

2. Due, J.F. and Fiedlsender, A.F.; "Government Finance, Economics of the Public Sector, Georgetown, Onterio, Richard D. Irwin, Inc. Hornewood, Illionois, Irwin Dorsey Ltd., 1973, p. 87.

3. Chellioh, Raja J. - Trends in Taxation in Developing countries, in Richard M. Bird and Oliver Oldman (edt.), "Readings on Taxation in Developing Countries", London, The Johns Hopkins University Press, 1975, p. 109.

4. Strictly speaking, an accurate measure of the marginal rate can be obtained only by using time-series data through a regression of tax revenue on income. It must be noted here, that our measures of marginal tax rate, based as it is on an observations at two points in time, are only rough estimate.

5. The effectiveness of indirect taxes stem from the hypothesis that such taxes are not difficult to administer, since a large proportion of the rural population derives its income in kind or in some other non-monetary form which is not easy for the assessment of tax purposes.

6. Harberger, Arnold C.; "Taxation, Resource Allocation and Welfare" in TheRole of Direct and Indirect Taxes in the Federal Revenue System, NBER and Brookings Institution, (Princeton University Press), (1964), pp. 25-81.

7. Lewis, A., "The Theory of Economic Growth, London, Richord D. Irwin, (1965), p. 403

8. Wallich, H.C. and Adler, J.H., Public Finance in Developing Country, Cambridge, M.I.T. Press, (1951), pp. 132-144.

9. Government of India, Report of the Taxation Enquiry Commission, Vol. I, p. 8.

10. Mathew, T.; Tax Policy : Some Aspects of Theory and Indian Experience, Delhi, KalyaniPublishers, (1975), pp. 93-94.

CHAPTER - VI
EMPIRICAL ANALYSIS

INTRODUCTION

An analysis of the compositional pattern of Orissa's tax revenues in the preceding chapter shows that on its own resource mobilization front, Orissa has failed to attain a desirable level of financial self-reliance in general and that with respect to its own taxing power in particular, its performance is not satisfactory. The resultant out come has been the increasing financial dependence of the state on the Union government in recent years. Further, the analysis carried out so far suggests that Orissa has made half-hearted tax efforts during the period under study, as a matter of which the observed anomalies in the state's tax system has remained the by product of the system.

THURST OF THE PROBLEM

All these observed trends noted above provides a solid ground for the necessity and the desirability of undertaking an analysis of the efficiency of the state tax measures. Accordingly, an attempt is made in this chapter to review the responsiveness and productivity of Orissa's tax systemin terms of the indicators noted in 1.2 of chapter 1, i.e. in terms of elasticity and buoyancy, to measure the relative degree of efficiency of the state's tax measures on the one hand and to indicate the extent to which additional tax efforts needed to increase the revenue of the government has been realized.

So, the related questions that are touched upon in thi context are:

(i) Whether the state of Orissa has succeeded in evolving a tax structure characterized by strong built-in-responsiveness of tax revenue with respect to state incomegrowth? If it is so, then to what extent it has relied on discretionary changes to improve tax yield? And,

(ii) Which of the individual taxes has fialed to accord a reasonable degree of responsiveness thereby giving rise to excessive dependendence of the state on the Centre?

This chapter which is the core of the study is divided into two parts. In section –I, the estimated buoyancy and elasticity of all the state's taxes of Orisaa taken together are analysed. And in sectionII similar estimates for all individual taxes are considered.

SECTION - I

BUOYANCY AND ELASTICITY OF ORISSA'S AGGREGATE TAXES

In this section, an attempt is made to measure the elasticity and buoyancy of all state's taxes of Orissa combined and then the same exercise was done for direct taxes, indirect taxes and shared taxes respectively.

Regression equations(49) and (50) are used to measure the buoyancy and elasticity coefficients respectively of the total tax revenues of the revenues of major tax groups. The equations are estimated for each of the selected items by the method of the least squares.

TAX BUOYANCY

The buoyancy of the tax system refers to the total response of the tax revenue resulting from automatic response (changes in state income and expenditure) and from discretionary changes (changes in tax base, rate etc.). This indicates that for a given percentage change in income, buoyancy measures the total percentage change in tax revenue attributable to these two combined effects.

Table-6.1 provides estimates of the buoyancy of Orissa's tax system. It is found that buoyancy coefficient of the state's total tax revenue is 1.3829. It implies that over the years, one percent increase in state income has resulted in 1.3829 percent increase in aggregate tax yield. Also, the buoyancy coefficient of state's own tax revenue is found to be 1.3949 during the period 1971-1982, which declined to 0.9615 for the period 1986-94. Again we found that shared tax revenue has a buoyancy coefficient of 1.5110 which is slightly greater than that of state's own total tax revenue. The buoyancy coefficients of direct and indirect taxes are found to be 1.2083 and 1.3563 respectively. A further decomposition of taxes into Taxes on Agricultural Land and Income, Taxes on Property and Capital Transactions and Taxes on Commodities and Services exhibited the highest buoyancy coefficient for Taxes on Commodities and Services (1.3826), followed by Taxes on Property and Capital Transactions (1.2161). Buoyancy coefficient for Tax group under Agricultural Land and Income came out to be the lowest. A higher buoyancy coefficient during the period under study signals that higher tax yields are the result of reasonable efforts of the government in modifying the tax parameters during that period.

While the elasticity of state's total own tax revenue came out as 1.3155 for the entire period, the same for the period 1976-87 is found to be 0.9460, which suggests that, at certain times the state resorted to a stringent discretionary measures to improve tax revenue collection. The elasticity of total indirect tax is found to be 1.3045, and on the other hand, the direct tax elasticity appeared to be inelastic. We may conclude by the numerical value evidence of elasticity that the substantial growth in tax revenue comes from indirect taxation. The low elasticity of direct taxes' revenue may be attributed to the low responsiveness of Agricultural Land and Income taxes and due to the non-uniformity of assessment of Agricultural Income.

A perusal of Table 6.1 also indicates that the aggregare response exhibited by the indirect tax group was always higher than the direct tax group and it is the direct taxes, where the failure to mobilize adequate resources is indicated. Coupled with a traditional agriculture, the Political gimmics has played a decisive role in keeping the tax burden of direct tax group at a lower level. The buoyancy coefficient of direct taxes is found to be 1.1603, while that of indirect taxes is 1.3563. Buoyancy of the direct tax group has not increased substantially over the plan periods. In fact, it has registered a decline from 1.2848, observed for the period 1981-1982 to 1991-92 to 0.7200, for the period 1986-87 to 1993-94. No doubt, the period from 1993-94 to 2001-2002 experienced an improvement, where the coefficient stood at 1.0638.

Further, the buoyancy coefficient of the total taxes on Agricultural Land and Income has recorded a substantial decline. The buoyancy coefficient of this particular tax group observed to be negative and stood at –0.8451 for the period 1961-62 to 1971-72 grew with a substantial pace to reach 1.4402 for the period 1971-72 to 1981-82. Further, it declined to 0.8763 for the period 1993-94 to 2001-2002. The overall buoyancy coefficient comes out to be 0.9957 for the entire period covered by the study. Whereas, the overall buoyancy coefficients for taxes on Property and Capital Transaction and that for taxes on Commodities and Services are found to be 1.2161 and 1.3826, respectively for the entire period of 40 years.

The low buoyancy coefficients of the Agricultural Tax group raise a question mark about the economic feasibility of these taxes in the overall tax system of the state. Given the economic significance that the buoyancy of taxes should be significantly higher than unity, the overall picture of Orissa's tax yields appears to be less satisfactory in the sense that, on the whole, the buoyancy coefficients of all the major tax groups have shown a declining trend in the recent years, especially in the Seventh and Eighth plan Periods (1986-87 to 1993-94).

TAX ELASTICITY

Tax elasticity measures the degree of automatic response of the tax yields to changes in state/national income after subtracting the discretionary response of a tax from the total response of the tax. A high tax elasticity over a period of time indicates the probable tax revenue that the government can raise with an unchanged tax rate and base of the tax or of the tax system. Elasticity coefficients of the total tax revenues as well as of sectoral tax groups are computed and presented in Table 6.2. The table indicates that, with respect to state income, the elasticity of state's total own tax revenue stands at 1.3155 for the period 1961-62 to 2001-02. Further, the elasticity coefficient is observed to have remained more or less stable throughout the period, except for the decade 1976-77 to 1986-87, where the elasticity coefficient is observed to be 0.9460. This suggests that the state has resorted to stringent discretionary measures to improve the tax yields during this particular period. The elasticities of the selected sector-wise tax groups give a divergent piicture. They are estimated to be 0.7231 for taxes on Agricultural Land and Income, as 0.9856 for taxes on Commodities and Services and as 1.1186 for taxes on Property and Capital Transactions. According to nature wise classification, they are ranging from 0.9564 for state's total direct tax revenues, to 1.3045 for state's total indirect taxes. This analysis substantia our earlier drawn inference that the direct taxes are less elastic than the indirect taxes in Orissa. The coefficients obtained for other taxes indicate that the elasticities of the taxes on Property and Capital Transactions and those of taxes on Commodities and Services are not differing to a significant extent in the statistical sense.

Table 6.2 further indicates that on the direct taxes front, the additional taxation effort carried out by the government is of negligible order. The difference between this group's buoyancy and elasticity is of the order of 0.2039. The results also indicate that the additional tax effort of the state is not of a remarkable order even in the case of indirect taxes. Against the recorded coefficient of 1.3045 for elasticity, this group's buoyancy coefficient is 1.3563. These minimal efforts of the state can therefore be identified as the other forces responsible for comparatively low difference obtained for the buoyancy and elasticity estimates (0.397) for Commodities and Services taxes. Further, the table indicates that the major reason for a relatively higher coefficient of buoyancy of Agricultural Taxes is the substantial efforts, put in by the state government in particular. This is substantiated by the fact that against the recorded coefficient of 0.7231 for elasticity, this group's buoyancy coefficient is 0.9957. The difference between these two coefficients is relatively high.

A comparison of the estimates given in Table II discloses that, over the period, the pattern of changes in tax yields is not uniform for all tax groups, while some tax groups have shown an improvement, the other tax groups disclosed an opposite pattern.

It may be mentioned here that the value of R^2 reported in all the estimates is rather high which is indicative of the fact that tax revenues are functionally related to state income.

SECTION - II

ELASTICITY AND BUOYANCY OF INDIVIDUAL STATE TAXES OF ORISSA

These elasticity coefficients presented in Table 6.2 forces us to wonder as to: which particular tax component is responsible for the observed efficiency/inefficiency of the above said major tax groups? An attempt is made to address this question by means of a further decomposition of the elasticities of the specified groups into the elasticities of the individual tax components under each group. The buoyancy and elasticity of Orissa's individual taxes are estimated by the same procedure as was done earlier in the case of all taxes combined. However, instead of using the State Domestic Product as the explanatory variable in all cases, the output of the particular sector of the economy is substituted where considered appropriate. For example, the base of agricultural income tax is not the entire State Product, but that portion of the State Domestic Product originating in the agriculture sector of the economy. In estimating the buoyancy and elasticity of the agricultural income tax, the State Domestic Product originating in the agricultural sector was taken as the explanatory variable. Elasticity and Buoyancy coefficients of the state's individual taxes are presented in Table 6.3. The explanatory variable used in each case is noted in the last column of the table.

It is evident from Table 6.3 that, of all taxes collected by the Orissa government, Electricity Duty is the most responsive to changes in State Income, in comparison to all other state taxes. The buoyancy and elasticity coefficients of Electricity Duty are found to be 1.71034 and 1.62231 respectively. Four other taxes exhibit buoyancy and elasticity coefficients greater than unity. These are the Stamp and Registration Duty, State Excise Tax, Vehicle Tax and Sales Tax. The performances of all these five taxes may be judged as satisfactory by both the buoyancy and elasticity criteria. On the other hand, the elasticities of taxes on agricultural sector are found to be small and insignificant; -0.0321 for Agricultural Income tax and 0.6321 for Land Revenue. The buoyancy coefficient of Land Revenue is worked out to be 1.1026. The major reason for higher degree of buoyancy of this particular tax is the substantial efforts put by the state government in rationalising the tax rate structure. The elasticity coefficient in case of Entertainment Tax is worked out to be 0.8976. The buoyancy coefficient of this particular tax incidentally happens to be lower than unity. Buoyancy and elasticity coefficients in case of taxes on Goods and Passengers are worked out to be negligible and hence are not reported. Thus, it may be inferred from the above findings that, the failures of thee government to accord a reasonable degree of built-in-flexibility to the Agricultural Income tax which has resulted in the poor performances of direct tax yields and Entertainment Tax and taxes on Goods and Passengers are to be identified as the two taxes, which are responsible for the dismal performance of the tax group namely taxes on Commodities and Services.

CONCLUSIONS

In this chapter, an attempt is made to estimate the coefficients of buoyancy and elasticity for Orissa's tax system. The taxation trend of Orissa's economy in early and late nineties had become more oriented towards indirect taxes. In this context, it can be argued that the inelastic nature of the Orissa's tax system on the direct tax front is an inherent characteristic resulting from the emergence of consumerism due to high propensity to consume, given the low level of income of the state. The results of the present study do not however provide sufficient empirical justification to this effect. Based on the overall trend that emerges from the analysis of elasticity and buoyancy of the major tax groups, the following inferences may be drawn.

On the direct tax front, the state has not succeeded in putting to track a tax structure characterized by a strong built–in-responsiveness of tax revenues with respect to state income. This is evident from a relatively greater buoyancy coefficient in relation to the elasticity coefficients, implying thereby, that the government has put in a greater degree of tax efforts to mobilize additional resources from this source. The low income elasticity of this particular group's taxes may be attributed to the factors like the loopholes in the tax laws, Lack of sincerety on the part of the government in its enforcement and the magnitude of tax avoidance and evasion.

In contrast to the direct tax group, indirect tax group exhibited a higher buoyancy and elasticity coefficients for the entire period covered by the study. This has been possible not only on account of the indirect taxes better responsiveness to the changes in rate of economic progress of the state, but also due to the substantial efforts made by the government to modify its tax structure to mobilize additional resources of its own.

And lastly, a further decomposition of taxes into three major groups namely, taxes on Agricultural Sector, taxes on Property and Capital Transaction and taxes on Commodities and Services gives some contrasting results. In case of taxes on Agricultural Sector and taxes on Commodities and Services, the elasticity coefficients are found to be rather low in comparison to that of taxes on Property and Capital Transactions. On these tax fronts, it may be stated that the state has not succeeded in evolving a rationalized tax structure for some of the taxes (pertaining to agricultural sector and commodities and service sector), which is characterized by a weak built-in-flexibility of tax revenue to changes in state income. As a result, the attainment of a reasonable degree of financial self –reliance has become a distinct reality for the state.

TABLE 6. 1

BUOYANCY ESTIMATES OF SELECTED GROUPS OF TAXES FOR THE PERIOD 1961-62 TO 2001-2002

	Tax Group	1961-62 to 1971-72		1966-67 to 1976-77		1971-72 to 1981-82		1976-77 to 1986-87		1981-82 to 1991-92		1986-87 to 1993-94		1993-94 to 2001-02		1961-62 to 2001-02	
		Buoyancy Coefficient	R^2	Buoyancy Coefficient	R^2	Buoyancy Coefficient	R^2	Buoyancy Coefficient	R^2	Buoyancy Coefficient	R^2	Buoyancy Coefficient	R^2	Buoyancy Coefficient	R^2	Buoyancy Coefficient	R^2
1.	All State's own Taxes	1.1042** (17.6220)	0.9718	1.3259** (7.8480)	0.8725	1.3949** (8.8630)	0.8933	1.1129** (16.5971)	0.9683	1.1606** (15.0749)	0.9679	0.9615** (15.5682)	0.9758	1.2901** (44.6711)	0.9436	1.3829** (56.5612)	0.9822
2.	Direct Taxes	0.4113** (5.4048)	0.7644	1.0341** (7.7949)	0.8709	1.2101** (10.4980)	0.9244	1.1863** (16.7147)	0.9687	1.2848** (8.4313)	0.8876	0.7200* (3.9283)	0.7200	1.1638 (39.2764)	0.8721	1.2083 (41.2640)	0.9548
3.	Indirect Taxes	1.4211** (21.8149)	0.9814	1.4642** (7.5205)	0.8627	1.4429** (8.3026)	0.8845	1.0948** (16.0193)	0.9660	1.1210** (16.2996)	0.9672	1.0217** (13.4599)	0.9679	1.1816 (19.5215)	0.9322	1.3563 (59.2231)	0.9126
4.	Shared Taxes	+	+	1.5571** (4.8725)	0.7251	1.6583** (4.8876)	0.7263	+	+	1.3012* (3.3604)	0.5564	1.7326** (-4.4489)	0.7673	1.6050 (27.3276)	0.9639	1.5110 (18.5633)	0.9645
5.	Taxes on Agri-Culture Land and Income	-0.5970** (-3.8982)	0.6345	0.6398* (2.6234)	0.4017	1.4402** (5.9186)	0.8239	1.1489** (12.4639)	0.7106	1.0439** (4.0215)	0.6424	0.8807 (2.1639)	0.1312	0.9652 (6.2136)	0. 9028	0.9957 (8.4316)	0.7327
6.	Taxes on Property and Capital Transac-tions	1.0658** (12.3796)	0.9445	1.2053** (9.7865)	0.9145	0.9755** (8.7860)	0.8955	1.0355** (13.9122)	0.9555	1.0107** (11.3191)	0.9343	0.8989** (7.0829)	0.8931	1.0216 (14.9820)	0.9693	1.2161 (60.5651)	0.9533
7.	Taxes on Commodities and Services	1.4207** (8.6054)	0.8445	1.3398** (7.1539)	0.8374	1.2205** (9.7027)	0.7840	1.0587** (12.9740)	0.9440	0.9825** (6.0320)	0.7280	0.9923** (4.9290)	0.7611	1.0234 (18.1350)	0.9123	1.3826 (26.4911)	0.9477

Note: Figures in the parentheses are t values. + Sign denotes that the equations have very negligible R^2

* Sign denotes that the coefficient is significant. ** Sign denotes that the coefficient is highly significant.

TABLE 6.2
ELASTICITY ESTIMATES OF SELECTED GROUPS OF TAXES FOR THE PERIOD 1961-62 TO 2001-2002

	Tax Group	1961-62 to 1971-72	1966-67 to 1976-77	1971-72 to 1981-82	1976-77 to 1986-87	1981-82 to 1991-92	1986-87 to 1993-94	1993-94 to 2001-02	1961-62 to 2001-02	1961-62 to 2001-02
		Elasticity Coefficient R^2	Elasticity Coefficient R^2	Elasticity Coefficient R^2	Elasticity Coefficient R^2	Elasticity Coefficient R^2	Elasticity Coefficient R^2	Elasticity Coefficient R^2	Elasticity Coefficient R^2	Net due to Discretionary Changes
1.	All State's own Taxes	1.2835** 0.9419 (12.0870)	1.3227** 0.9140 (9.7826)	1.1968** 0.8891 (8.4981)	0.9460* 0.9205 (10.2116)	1.0200** 0.9752 (18.8330)	1.2681** 0.9803 (17.3026)	1.4733 0.8312 (11.0116)	1.3155 0.9693 (43.0641)	0.0674
2.	Direct Taxes	0.3986** 0.8821 (8.2079)	0.9323** 0.8626 (7.5168)	1.1318** 0.9270 (10.6981)	0.8222** 0.9690 (16.7750)	0.9961** 0.9305 (10.9843)	0.8870* 0.8979 (7.2678)	0.9861 0.9179 (12.5437)	0.9564 0.9347 (34.6322)	0.2519
3.	Indirect Taxes	1.7705** 0.9403 (11.9139)	1.4786** 0.8882 (8.4585)	1.2140** 0.8678 (8.3026)	0.9825** 0.8990 (8.9621)	1.0238** 0.9628 (15.2707)	1.4089** 0.9844 (19.4735)	1.3169 0.8344 (18.4962)	1.3045 0.9577 (32.6789)	0.0518
4.	Taxes on Agri-Culture Land and Income	-0.8451* 0.6761 (-4.2137)	0.4121* 0.3128 (2.1242)	1.1617** 0.7659 (5.2780)	0.7618** 0.8964 (9.4012)	1.1768** 0.6471 (4.0626)	+ +	0.3211 0.8672 (1.7613)	0.7231 0.5701 (7.1369)	0.2726
5.	Taxes on Property and Capital Transac-tions	1.1411** 0.9040 (9.2090)	1.2068** 0.9144 (9.8097)	0.9799** 0.8831 (8.2483)	0.9553** 0.9504 (13.1112)	0.9967** 0.9212 (10.2576)	0.9126** 0.8713 (6.3752)	0.9962 0.9148 (14.3172)	1.1186 0.9634 (52.1673)	0.0975
6.	Taxes on Commodities and Services	1.6825** 0.7977 (8.2388)	1.2153** 0.7471 (6.5804)	1.1105** 0.8027 (6.7638)	0.7315** 0.7228 (5.1781)	1.0073** 0.8459 (6.8345)	0.6879** 0.8818 (7.2029)	1.0213 0.8932 (6.9231)	0.9856 0.8547 (28.6315)	0.397

Note: Figures in the parentheses are t values. + Sign denotes that the equations have very negligible R^2

*Sign denotes that the coefficient is significant. ** Sign denotes that the coefficient is Highly significant

TABLE 6. 3

BUOYANCY, ELASTICITY AND RELATED STATISTICS OF STATES'S TAXES IN ORISSA FOR 1961-62 TO 2001-2002

Tax Group		1961-62 to 1971-72		1971-72 to 1981-82		1981-82 to 1991-92		1991-92 to 2001-02		1961-62 to 2001-02		1961-62 to 2001-02		
		Coefficient of Buoyancy(B) & Elesticity(E)	R^2	Coefficient of Buoyancy(B) & Elesticity(E)	R^2	Coefficient of Buoyancy(B) & Elesticity(E)	R^2	Coefficient of Buoyancy(B) & Elesticity(E)	R^2	Coefficient of Buoyancy(B) & Elesticity(E)	R^2	Net due to Discretionary Measures		Explanatory Variable
	(1)	(2)	(3)	(4)	(5)	(6)	(7)	(8)	(9)	(10)	(11)	(12)	(13)	(14)
1.	Land Revenue	B:-0.5973 (-3.9133)	0.6298	B:-1.4904 (6.0746)	0.8039	B:-1.3439 (4.0215)	0.6424	B:-1.4729 (6.8613)	0.8956	B:1.1926 (14.3627)	0.9032	0.7863		Net State Domestic Product (NSDP)
		E:-0.8553 (-4.1700)	0.6890	E:-1.1818 (5.4990)	0.7707	E:-1.1768 (4.0626)	0.6471	E:-1.2035 (5.6982)	0.7693	E:0.7863 (5.6219)	0.5280			Originating in Agricultural Sector
2.	Agricultural	B: +	+	B:-0.0902 (-3.2530)	0.5407	B: +	+	B:-0.0624 (-4.3125)	0.5832	B:-0.0491 (-7.6386)	0.5786	—		NSDP originating
		E: +	+	E:-0.0808 (-2.8744)	0.4786	E: +	+	E:-0.0723 (-3.6217)	0.6202	E:-0.0321 (-5.6537)	0.5176			in agriculturaltural Sector
3.	Stamp Duty	B:1.0658 (12.3796)	0.9445	B:0.9755 (8.7860)	0.8955	B:1.0107 (11.3191)	0.9346	B:1.2356 (13.1698)	0.9127	B:1.3051 (52.6355)	0.9820	0.2595		NSDP
		E:1.0411 (9.2090)	0.9040	E:0.9699 (8.0248)	0.8831	E:0.9967 (10.2576)	0.9212	E:1.0203 (8.2130)	0.7763	E:1.0456 (47.1745)	0.9402			
4.	State Excise Duty	B:1.4771 (7.7837)	0.8706	B:0.7391 (10.8460)	0.9289	B:1.2305 (14.1142)	0.9567	B:1.3568 (15.5216)	0.8247	B:1.1564 (33.1043)	0.9549	0.0843		NSDP
		E:1.0958 (9.3790)	0.9071	E:0.5639 (7.6376)	0.8660	E:1.1922 (19.5890)	0.9770	E:1.2050 (21.6233)	0.9100	E:1.0721 (47.3628)	0.9621			
5.	Vehicle Tax	B:1.2676 (9.7236)	0.9130	B:1.2467 (11.2841)	0.9339	B:1.2748 (9.8380)	0.9149	B:1.2856 (10.5388)	0.9239	B:1.3962 (56.6728)	0.8322	0.1929		NSDP
		E:1.0400 (21.1121)	0.9802	E:1.2160 (10.6686)	0.9267	E:0.8203 (8.9337)	0.8986	E:0.9897 (9.6210)	0.9481	E:1.2033 (35.5216)	0.7840			

(Condt...)

	(1)	(2)	(3)	(4)	(5)	(6)	(7)	(8)	(9)	(10)	(11)	(12)	(13)	(14)
6.	Electricity Duty	B:4.4759 (8.3743)	0.8862	B:1.9064 (7.2661)	0.8543	B:1.0599 (1.5196)	0.6941	B:1.8604 (8.3662)	0.7960	B:1.9213 (19.5782)	0.9670	0.2509		NSDP
		E:3.2706 (5.9456)	0.7970	E:1.4211 (5.5450)	0.7735	E:0.9224 (3.2903)	0.5460	E:1.0123 (10.6254)	0.8571	E:1.6704 (12.8675)	0.9664			
7.	Entertainment Tax	B:1.1746 (11.2500)	0.9336	B:1.6040 (7.4615)	0.8608	B:0.8872 (2.1852)	0.1334	B:1.0247 (5.6231)		B:1.2138 (18.2632)	0.7703			
		E:0.9692 (9.5076)	0.9094	E:1.3545 (4.1596)	0.6577	E:0.5417 (1.7755)	0.0923	E:0.8629 (2.8762)		E:0.8976 (8.1121)	0.9056			
8.	Sales Tax	B:1.7265 (12.2496)	0.9434	B:1.4970 (8.2389)	0.8829	B:1.1638 (17.0140)	0.9698	B:1.3562 (18.1342)		B:1.5154 (17.2985)	0.9671			
		E:1.3682 (15.7020)	0.9647	E:1.2812 (6.8351)	0.8384	E:1.0560 (17.7900)	0.9723	E:1.1027 (26.2356)		E:1.3231 (20.3981)	0.8704			
9.	Taxes on Goods and Passengers	B:0.5155 (2.5780)	0.4247	B:0.7989 (5.1580)	0.7472	B: +	+	B: +		B: +		0.3162		NSDP
		E:0.1787 (1.7963)	0.2639	E:0.3605 (1.7353)	0.2507	E: +	+	E: +		E: +		0.1923		NSDP

Note: Figures in the parentheses are t values. + Equations have very negligible R^2 * = significant. ** =

CHAPTER - VII

CONCLUSION

MAJOR FINDINGS

In the foregoing chapters, an attempt was made to highlight the various aspects of Orissa's tax system with a motive to indicate the spheres in which problems have arisen and solutions are necessary. In doing this,although we have touched upon various aspects of the problem, we have not gone in great detail, into the considerable statistical material that have been presented in the tables. The reason is, our objective has been to emphasize on the responsiveness and productivity of Orissa's tax system and keep away from exercises which will contradict the scheme of the present work. To this extent the study can be said to be exhaustive in the raising of issues of various aspects of taxation but not exhaustive in treating them.

With these limitations in mind, an attempt is made in the following paragraphs to give a comprehensive account of the major findings of our study. The important findings of the study are as follows:

(i) One of the most diturbing features of state finance that emerges from the study is the growing volume of revenue deficits in recent years. The continuous outspacing of the growth of revenues both in the eighties and nineties, has led to serious deterioration in the State's budgetary positions, from a surplus of

1.32 percent of Net State Domestic Product in the mid seventies (i.e., in the 1977-78) to a deficit of about 1.22 percent of Net State Domestic Product in 1993-94. In absolute terms, the net revenue deficits in 1993-94 was close to Rs. 181.60 crores.

(ii) Since 1982-83, dis-saving has been showing large increases year after year mainly due to very high growth of revenue expenditures. The increase in expenditures has been particularly alarming in 1984-85, when it grew at an average rate of 14.63 percent per annum. What is more, with the interest liability itself growing at 23.29 percent per year, expenditure growth has become self-propelling.

(iii) Thus, the higher growth of revenue expenditure in relation to the growth of revenue receipts has created an explosive cycle of expenditure growth. The use of borrowed funds for meeting revenue expenditure, while increasing interest liability does not create corresponding sources of revenue. In addition, even the borrowed funds used for capital spending are not efficiently utilized. Due to this, the State's gross interest payments during the decade of 1990's grew at the average annual rate of 47.23 percent. Clearly, such a high growth rate of interest payment expenditure is unsustainable in an under developed state like Orissa.

(iv) If, we assume that the observed trend in revenue expenditures will continue into the future in the medium term then, in order to phase out the revenue deficits into the next four years, i.e., by 1998-99, the revenue growth would have to accelerated by almost 3.36 percentage points to 10.02 percent per annum. This is indeed a unjustified estimation and therefore, immediate remedial measures either to increase the tax efforts or to compress the expenditures must be undertaken.

(v) The increasing State Income over a period of time has been out-paced by the increasing state's own tax revenue and much more so, by total tax revenue.

(vi) The role of the State's own tax revenue as an element of State Income over the period has not been commensurate with the expected or likely drive for additional taxation as a source of revenue for the State. This is so because of the fact, that the percentage share of the State's own tax revenue in State Income has increased at a much slower pace than the pace ascribed to total tax revenue.

(vii) If, we visualize tax-income ratio as a simplest measure of tax burden or, sacrifice, then the result of our analysis showed that in absolute terms, state's tax burden has almost doubled and hence going for further taxation would be objectionable. But in a relative sense (i.e.; from the angle of total tax revenue), the concept of tax burden would be more meaningful and in this comparison, Orissa emerges rather poorly.

(viii) The overall trends of revenue from taxation in Orissa show a steady increase over all the plan periods covered by the study. But, a close examination of these especially with relation to state income discloses that the revenues' built-in-flexibility has not improved at all. It was of the order of 1.3227 for the period of 1966-67 to 1976-77 and 1.020 for the period 1981-82 to 1991-92. What appears from the results is that the latter years' changed composition of taxation in particular has not facilitated much to improve the automatic growth o tax receipts.

(ix) The tax system since the beginning of the sixth plan in particular is heavily oriented towards the urban and modern sectors of the economy and has neglected the rural and the agricultural sectors. This follows from the declining importance of agricultural (particularly agricultural income tax) Taxes, and the increasing importance of taxes on property and capital transactions and state's sales tax. But, the accepted logic seems to be that a rise in taxation ought to come from areas where increments in income take place. For some years, the terms of trade have moved heavily in favour of the rural sector. This is clear from the sustained upward movement of the money incomes of the dominant sector of rural economy, viz., the agricultural sector, even in the years of excessive drought. And now that the agricultural revolution appears to be overtaking the state economy, the incomes in rural sector tend to rise sharply. Further, the impression is that the additional incomes are largely accruing to households with medium and large land-holdings. This primafacie suggests the presence of considerable reserves of income in the rural sector and this could be utilised to finance their development requirements in particular, of the agricultural sector.

(x) Over the planning years, the development of public investments into the development of agriculture has increased to substantial extent. And these large deployments have helped raising the incomes of agriculturists. Then, one can quite naturally expect that the agriculturists' contribution to the exchequer has to increase substantially. Contrary to this expectation, it is observed that the contribution of the agricultural sector has remained more or less stagnant and it infact has shrunk to almost insignificant proportion of income from agriculture, etc. This also substantiates the need for having a fresh look at the plausible means of bringing the agriculturists into the orbit of tax net in a more objective way.

(xi) The main drawback of the present day land revenue system in Orissa is that, it fails to take into consideration the differences in the productivity of land. This in the presence of various factors, such as different tenurial system and the levels of productivity has led to diminish the progressiveness of the tax system. A simple way of raising more revenue through direct taxation of agriculture would be to levy surcharge on land revenue making its incidence a multiple of what it is now. The replacement of land revenue by agricultural holding tax, as suggested by Raj committee, can also bring about a higher level of progressiveness into the tax system and thereby improve automatic response of agricultural taxes to the rising income of the sector.

(xii) The results also disclose that the low elasticities of some of the state taxes have to be explained interms of their low rate responses, i.e., the factors which would fall mostly within the ambit of tax administration authorities.

(xiii) The most unfortunate feature of the state's land revenue and agricultural income tax structure is that it has been erratic and unstable in base and rate schedules. Added to this, the changes in levy surcharges such as Nistar cess and Land cess, etc., have made the computation of tax payer's tax liability a difficult task. This evidently indicates the lack of proper thought and consideration before a measure is brought on to the Statute book. The factors which can be considered for improving elasticity of agricultural income tax comprise, the revision of exemptions structure, enhancement of tax rates at all levels of income, and the re-orientation of the definition of income currently being used for arriving at taxable income.

(xiv) Similarly, an examination of the direct tax on agricultural land has not shown itself to be "effective" instrument of resource mobilization. The income elasticity and buoyancy of this tax has been comparatively low and in addition owing to the `loopholes' in the law and perhaps laxity in its enforcement, the magnitude of tax avoidance and evasion has been enormous, with the result that, this tax has shrunk both in its dimension and denomination.

(xv) The taxation trend of Orissa's economy in recent years has become more and more oriented towards indirect and consumption taxes. This trend by itself has been sought as on explanation for low elasticity of Orissa's direct tax system. To be more specific, it may be mentioned that the inelastic nature of Orissa's direct tax structure is an inherent characteristic resulting from heavy reliance placed on indirect taxes. The results of present study do not, however, provide adequate empirical justification to this account. They, rather, disclose that indirect taxes in general contain better automatic growth potentialities.

(xvi) The wide differences between the elasticity and buoyancy estimates of entertainment tax, vehicle tax suggests that increase in revenue productivity has come through new tax measures. The difference is greater in the case of entertainment tax. It may, however, be noted that the major factor which appears to have acted as a deterrent to the growth of these taxes, are the low rate elasticities of these taxes. This, in a way suggests the need for the rationalization of these taxes.

(xvii) As an instrument of resource mobilization, the indirect levy of sales tax has been much more productive than all other taxes and, further that the levy world have been helpful also as a means of curtailing consumption. The sales tax shown a high degree of income elasticity and buoyancy with a result that it has come to occupy pride of place, so to say, among the numerous tax measures.

(xviii) An analysis of elasticity and buoyancy estimates of State's excise duty indicated that no significant discretionary changes have taken place in the case of the state on this account. It means, the growth in the receipts has come mainly through increased liquor consumption and to some extent due to tightened administrative controls. A close analysis of the said tax reveals that the elasticity coefficient has shown a declining trend over the periods covered by our study. This declining trend indicates the fact that the excise duty which once was the most productive means of revenue has lost its importance and are currently being used more for the purposes of regulating the consumption of liquor and narcotics than that of resource mobilization.

From the above findings, it is clear that, as an instrument of resource mobilization, fiscal policy in general and the taxation policy of the State Government in particular has not been a remarkable success. From the available evidence, it is seen that taxation policy of the State both through its direct and indirect levies has not able to bring about any significant increase in the overall resource mobilization programme to meet its ever increasing publicexpenditure programmes. As a result of which the dependence of the state on the centre is on the increase in recent years.

POLICY IMPLICATION

It is always possible to devise a suitable system of taxation where the existing weakness can be removed.

Taking into account the above factors, it is possible to suggest the following considerations for evolving a suitable system of taxation.

Given the high proportion of consumption expenditure in total State Domestic Product, the relative share of Government revenues has to be increased mainly by manipulating consumption activities. Here, the emphasis will have to be not much on reducing existing consumption expenditure all along the line as on reducing additional consumption corresponding to additional income. Clearly, therefore, what we argue is that the incidence of taxation should be more on those sectors which, in the development process, enjoy a faster growth of incomes.

Given the basic objectives, the following elements may be mentioned as desirable for being incorporated in a satisfactory policy of taxation : On the agricultural taxation front. (i) It may be advisable to have a rate structure such that it would not impose an unwiedly burden on the agriculturists, but at the same time would bring within the tax net as large a number of agriculturists as are able to pay the tax without undue distress, (ii) The standard settlements should be periodically revised every five to seven years so as to make the system elastic with respect to changing economic conditions, and (iii) Since, there exists a system of differential taxation of agricultural and non-agricultural incomes, which disturbs the natural flow of resources between sectors, we may suggest a unified income tax structure for both agricultural and non-agricultural incomes we believe that this will help in regulating the intersectoral flow of resources.

On the indirect taxation front, we may stress on the Rationalisation of simplification of the tax structure in order to compel it to be more buoyant and elastic than its original level. In this regards, certain measures which needs immediate attention are : (i) Ways have to be found to reduce the number of sales tax rate and levy uniform tax rates in respect of some important commodities. The number of tax rates should be brought down to atleast two or three in the course of next two years and this will nodoubt reduce both administrative and compliance costs significantly. No doubt this particular point has been taken care by newly introduced unified value Added Tax (VAT). (ii) Measures should be taken to relieve the burden of the tax on inputs through a system of tax credits. And, with better information system, perhaps attempt could be made to extend the tax base to the stages beyond manufacturing on the principle of "value added".

(iii) The sales tax incentives given for industrialisation in the state need to be rationalised (iv) The other two taxes which need to be rationalised are the entertainment tax and stamps and Registration Duty. The levy of the stamp duties at very high rates of 15 to 20 percent has resulted in substantial under valuation of immovable property. This has led to investments in real estates an important source of underground economy. The same amount of tax could perhaps be collected by reducing the tax rate, and lastly, (v) the entertainment tax should be brought under stricter tax compliance in order to make it more buoyant and elastic.

If we will be allowed to compress our arguments in this work into one single sentence, it would be that the direct and indirect tax systems of the state have to be integrated and treated in such a way that each can play the role expected of it without any economic and political hassles. In the absence of a vibrant economy, the integration will be dependent upon the extent to which the state accords a reasonable degree of built-in-flexibility in its tax structure. In this sense, the problem of taxation is not one to be solved by sheer financial expertise but by the strong political will of the government keeping aside its popular sovereignty and pursuing a policy of command polity in formulating its fiscal policy measures. Ultimately formulation of fiscal policy measures remains a logical off shoot of the political ideology of the political party in power Therefore; every effort should be taken by the government to see to the fact that the economic values should take an edge over the political value in order to have rationality component in the tax system. The very outlook on the part of the state machinery can make it possible for them to over come the problem of resource mobilisation which has been demanding and continue to demand attention in the state scene for all times to come. Therefore, political tolerance to expended economic activities coupled with a rational and consistent tax regime is the only way out in mobilizing adequate tax revenue carrying out developmental programs in the states.

BIBLIOGRAPHY

Auld, D.A.L., 'Automatic Fiscal Stabilizers : Problems of Identification and Measurement,' *Journal of Public Finance*, Vol. 26, No. 4, (1971).

Bagchi, A. and Sen, T., Kerala's Revenue Potential : Projections for 1990-95, National Institute of Public Finance and Policy, (1989).

Bagchi Amaresh and Rao, M. Govnda., *Elasticity of Non-Corporate Income Tax in India, in Economic and Political Weekly*, Vol. 17, (Sept. 1982), pp. 1452-58.

Bahl, Roy W., *A Regression Approach to Tax Effort and Tax Ratio Analysis*, in I.M.F. Staff Papers, (Nov. 1971).

Bansal, R.K.; Raising Additional Resources in the States, New Delhi, Atlantic Publishers and Distributors, (1988).

Benjamin Higgins, Economic Development : Principles, Problems and Policies, Central Book Depot, Allahabad, (1966).

Bez, K.; Quantitative Techniques in Economics, New Delhi, Kalyani Publishers, (1990).

Bird, R.M. and Oldman, O. (eds.), Readings on Taxation in Developing Countries, John Hopkins Press, (1972).

Bird, R.M., *Assessing Tax Performance in Developing Countries, A Critical Review of the Literature, in Finanzarchiy*, Vol. 14, (1976), pp. 246-65.

Bird, Richard M. and Head, John G. (eds.), *Modern Fiscal Issues*, Toronto, University of Toronto Press, (1972).

Bretherton, R.F., *The Sensitivity of Taxes to Fluctuations of Trade, in Econometrica*, Vol. V (1937), p. 171.

Byrne, William J., *The Elasticity of the Tax System of Zambia 1966-1977 in World Development*, Vol. II, (Feb. 1983), pp. 153-62.

Chelliah, R.J., Bass, H.J. and Kelly, M.R., *Tax Ratios and Tax Efforts in Developing Countries*, in I.M.F. Staff Papers, (March, 1975).

Chelliah, Raja J. and Sinha, Narian; *Measurement of Tax Effort of State Government 1973-1976*, New Delhi, National Institute of Public Finance and Policy, (1983).

Chelliah, R.J., *Fiscal Policy in Underdeveloped Countries*, Bombay, George Allen and Unwin (Inida) Private Limited (1969).

Choudhury, Nurun N., *A Study of the Elasticity of the West Malaysian Income Tax System*, in I.M.F. Staff Papers, vol. 22, (July 1975), pp. 494-509.

Cohen, Leo J., *An Empirical Measurement of the Built- in flexibility of the Individual Income Tax*, American Economic Review, Papers and Proceedings, (1959).

Cutt, J., *Taxation and Economic Development*, Delhi, Vikash Publications, (1969).

Das, S.K.; *Dynamics of Taxation in A Developing Economy (with special reference to Assam) : 1964-65 to 1978-79*, Guwahati, Omson Publication, (1987).

Dorrence Graime S., *The Effects of Inflation or Economic Development*, I.M.F. Staff Paper, Vol. 17, No 2, (March 1963)

Douglas, M; *Taxable Capacity and British and Canadian Experience*, in Limits of Taxable Capacity (Princeton, N.J., Tax Institute, Inc. (1953).

Due, J.F. and Fiedlsender, A.F.; *Government Finance : Economics of the Public Sector*, Richard d. Irwin, Inc. Hornewood, Illionois, Irwin Dorsey Limited, Georgetown, Onterio, (1973).

Edelberg, V., Flexibility of the Yield of Taxation : Some Econometric Investigation', *Journal of the Royal Statistical Society*, Part-II, (1940).

Gandhi, Ved. P., *Some Aspects of India's Tax Structure*, Bombay, Vora and Co. Publishers Pvt. Ltd. (1970).

Goode, R.B., *Taxation and Economic Development*, in Morgan, T.; Betz, F.W.; and Choudhary, N. (eds); Readings in Economic Development, Belmont; Wordsworth Publishing Co., (1963).

Government of India - *Reports of the Indirect Taxation Enquiry Committee*, Part-II (Jan. 1978), p. 399

Government of India - *Taxation Enquiry Commission Report*, Vol. III, (1954).

Government of Orissa; An Economic-cum Purpose Classification of the Orissa Government Budget, 1980-81 to 1989-90, Bhubneswar, *Directorate of Economic and Statistics*, (1992).

Government of Orissa; *Statistical Abstract of Orissa*, Cuttack, Orissa Government Press, (1968-1991).

Government of Orissa; *Economic Survey of Orissa*, Cuttack, Orissa Government Press, (1970-1993).

Government of Orissa; *Orissa Budget in Brued*, Cuttack, Orissa Government Press, (1968-1994).

Government of Orissa; *Statistical Outline of Orissa*, Cuttack, Orissa Government Press, (1968-1992).

Government of Orissa; *An Economic and Functional Classification of Orissa Budget*, Cuttack, Orissa Government Press, (1970-1994).

Government of Orissa; Estimates of State Domestic Product

1950-51 to 1988-89, Bhubneswar, *Directorate of Economics and Statistics.*

Government of Orissa; *Conspectus of Orissa Budget, 1936-37 to 1973-74,* Cuttack, Orissa Government Press, (1974).

Government of Orissa; *Notes on Subsidiary Points Presented to Finance Commission*, Cuttack, Government of Orissa Press, (1964).

Government of Orissa; *Notes on Subsidiary Points Presented to Fifth Finance Commission;* Cuttack, Government of Orissa Press, (1968).

Government of Orissa; *Notes on Subsidiary Points Presented to Sixth Finance Commission,* Cuttack, Government of Orissa Press, (1972).

Government of Orissa; *Notes on Subsidiary Points Presented to Seventh Finance Commission,* Cuttack, Government of Orissa Press, (1978).

Government of Orissa; *Notes on Subsidiary Points Presented to Eighth Finance Commission,* Cuttack, Government of Orissa Press, (1983).

Government of Orissa; *Notes on Subsidiary Points Presented to Ninth Finance Commission,* Cuttack, Government of Orissa Press, (1988).

Government of Orissa; *Notes on Subsidiary Points Presented to Tenth Finance Commission,* Cuttack, Government of Orissa Press, (1993).

Groves, H.M. and Khan, C.H., "The stability of state and Local Tax Yields', *American Economic Review,* Vol. 41, (March, 1952).

Herberger, Arnold C., *Taxation, Resource Allocation and Welfare', in The Role of Direct and Indirect Taxes in the Federal Revenue System,* NBER and Brookings Institution, Princeton University Press, (1964).

Hariss, R., *Income and Sales Taxes* : The 1970 Outlook for

States and Localities, Chicago, The Council of State Government, (1968).

Hicks, U.K., *Finances of British Government* : 1920-36, London, Oxford University Press, (1938).

Jain, M.M.; 'Income Elasticity of Indian Tax Structure 1955-56 to 1965-66', *Economic and Political Weekly*, Vol. IV, No. 18, (May3, 1969).

Joseph A. Pechman, Yield of Individual Income Tax During a Recersion : Policy to Combet Depression, Princeton, Princeton University Press, (1953).

Kaldor, Nicholas; *Taxation for Economic Development*, Journal of Modern African Studies, vol. 1 (1963)

Khadye, I.K., *The Responsiveness in India, 1960-61 to 1978-79', in R.B.I.* Occasional Papers, Vol. 2, No. I, (June 1981), p. 34.

Lakdawala, D.T., and Nambiar, K.V., *Commodity Taxation in India*, Ahmedabad, Sardar Patel Institute of Economic and Social Research, (1972).

Lakdawala, D.T. and Khambadkune; 'The Sensitivity of Central Taxes : 1948-49 to 1954-55', *The Economic Weekly*, December 5th, (1959), pp. 1933-1940.

Lakdwala, D.T., *Justice in Taxation in India*, Bombay, Vora and Co. Publishers Pvt. Ltd., (1970).

Legler, J.B. and Shapiro, P., The Responsiveness of State Tax Revenue to Economic Growth', *National Tax Journal*, Vol. 21, No. 1, March 1968, Richard A. Musgrave, The Theory of Public Finance, Mc-Graw-Hill Book Co., New York, (1959).

Lewis, W. Jr., *Federal Fiscal Policy in The Post War Recersions*, Washigton, D.C. Bar. Brookings Institution, (1962).

Lewis, A., *The Theory of Economic Growth*, London, Richard D. Irwin, (1965).

Lotz, J.R. and Morss, E.R. *Measuring Tax Effort in Developing Countries*, in I.M.F. Staff Papers, (Nov. 1967).

Machiraju, H.R., *Fiscal Policy For Equitable Growth*, Delhi, The Macmillan Co. of India Ltd., (1977).

Mansfield, C.Y., *'Elasticity and Buoyancy of a Tax System : A Method Applied to Parguay'*, in I.M.F. Staff Papers, vol. 19, No. 2, (July 1972), p. 427.

Mathew, T., *Tax Policy : Some Aspects of Theory and Indian Experience*, Delhi, Kalyani Publishers, (1974).

Mathew, T., *Fiscal Policy in the Planned Economy in India*, (Bokhale Endowment Lectures, University of Madras, 1959), Delhi, S. Chand and Co., (1960).

Mathew, T., Economic Objectives and Tax Expenditure Policies of India during 1950-70, New Delhi, *Economic and Scientific Foundation*, (1974).

Mathew, T., 'Fiscal Policy in India, 1950-80', in J.N. Mongia (Ed.), *India's Economic Policies*, Allied Publishers, New Deli, (1980).

Mathew, T., *Fiscal and Monetary Policies in India*, in Indian Law Institute (ed.), Government Resolution of Private Enterprise, N.M. Tripathy Pvt. Ltd., Bombay, (1971).

Mathew, T., 'Fiscal Illusion : *The Political Economy of Resource Mobilization*, Economic Times, New Delhi, Sect. 11 & 19, (1971).

Mathew, T., *Economics of Public Expenditure*, Bombay, Vora & Co. Publishers Pvt. Ltd., (1972).

Maxwell, J.A., *Fiscal Policy*, Henry Holt and Co. New York 1955.

Mishra, B., *Agricultural Taxation in Orissa*, 1970-80, Unpublished M. Phil Thesis, NEHU, (1985).

Nambiar, K.V. and Rao, M. Govinda,; Tax Performance of State', *Economic and Political Weekly*, Vol. VII, No. 21, (May 20. 1972).

Pershad, H., *Indian Taxation during World War II*, Bombay, Allied Publishers Pvt. Lt. (1964).

Prest, A.R., *The Sensitivity of the Yield of the Personal Income Tax in the United Kingdom, in Economic Journal*, Vol. 72 (Sept. 1969), pp. 576-596.

Rao, V.G., *The Responsiveness of the Indian Tax System 1960-61 to 1973-74*, Banglore, Allied Publishers Pvt. Ltd. (1970).

Rao, M.G.; *Proposal for State LEvel Budgetary Reforms*, Paper presented at IIDS Seminar on Fiscal Discipline and Fiscal Consolidation at the Central and State level IIDS, Calcutta, (February 19, 1992) (mimeo).

Rao, K.B.K.; *Does the Indian Tax Policy Have a Rational* Margin, Vol. 4, No. 3, (April 1972).

Rao, K.B.K.; *Income Elasticity of Central and State Taxes*, Margin, Vol. 1, No. 3, (April 1969).

Rao, M. Govinda; 'Economic and Political Determinants of Sales Tax Revenue : A Case Study of Four State', *Economic and Political Weekly*, Vol. XIV, No. 47, (Nov. 24, 1979).

Ray C.L., *A Note on State Stability Criteria', National Tax Journal*, Vol. 19, No. 2, (June 1966).

Reddy, K.N.; *Inter-State Tax Effort, Economic and Political Weekly*, Vol. X, No. 50, (Dec. 13, 1975).

Richard, M. Bird, 'Public Finance and Inequality', *Finance and Development*, (March, 1947).

Richard A. Musgrave and Miller, *Built in Flexibility, American Economic Review*, (March, 1948), Reprint in Readings in Fiscal Policy, American Economic Association.

Richard, A. Musgrave; *The Theory of Public Finance* (ISE), The Mc. Graw-Hill Book Company, (1961).

Sahota, G.S., *Indian Tax Structure and Economic Development*, Bombay, Asia Publishing House (1961).

Singer, N.M., The use of dummy Variables in Estimating the

Income Elasticity of State Income Tax Revenues', *National Tax Journal,* Vol. 21, No. 2, (June, 1968).

Singer, N.M., 'Estimating State Income Tax Revenues : A New Approach', *Review of Economic and Statistics,* Vol. 52, (September, 1970).

Sinharay, M., *On Government Expenditure and Economic Development of India, Economic Studies,* (March, 1964), pp. 459-466.

Suman, H.N.P.S., *Direct Taxation and Economic Development in India,* New Delhi, Sterling Publishers Pvt. Ltd. (1974).

Sury, M.M., *Buoyancy and Elasticity of Union Excise Revenue in India 1950-51 to 1980-81,* Unpublished Ph.D. Thesis, University of Delhi, (1985).

T. Barna, *Redistribution of Income through PublicFinance,* Oxford Clareden Press, (1945).

Thimmaaiah, G., *Perspectives on Tax Design and Tax Reforms,* New Delhi, Asia Publishing House, (1984).

Venkataraman, K., *State's Finances in India, London,* George Allen and Unwin Ltd. (1968).

Venkataraman, K., *Local Finance in Perspective,* Bombay, Asia Publishing House (1965).

Wallich, H.C. and Adler, J.H.; *Public Finance in Developing Country,* Cambridge, M.I.T. Press, (1951).

Wasylenko, M. *Estimating the Elasticity of State Personal Income Taxes, National Tax Journal,* Vol. 28, No. 1, (March, 1975).

Wieford, D.S. and Wieford, W.T., *Estimates of Revenue Elasticity and Buoyancy in Central America,* 1955-1974', in J.F.J. Toye, Taxation and Economic Development, (London, Aug. 1978), pp. 83-101.

Wilford, W.T., 'State Tax Stability Criteria and the Revenue Income Elasticity Coefficient Reconsidered', *National Tax Journal,* Vol. 18, No. 3, (September, 1965).

INDEX

❑❑❑